DEMI VEG
The new style of cookery that is

NOT QUITE VEGETARIAN

Exciting recipes for our changing lifestyle

DEMI VEG
The new style of cookery that is

NOT QUITE VEGETARIAN

Exciting recipes for our changing lifestyle

RICHARD CAWLEY

Photography by
Trevor Richards

ORBIS · LONDON

For my parents

Notes

All recipes serve 6 people, unless otherwise stated.

Throughout, size 3 eggs are used.

Flour refers to plain or all-purpose flour.

Preparation times are approximate and will vary according to the individual cook's skill and speed.

Ovens should be preheated to the specified temperature.

All spoon measures are level, unless otherwise stated.

Follow one system of measures — they are not interchangeable.

Note to Australian readers: The Australian tablespoon has been converted to 20ml, which is larger than the tablespoon used in this book, and therefore 3 level teaspoons should be used where instructed to use 1 tablespoon.

First published in 1986 by
Orbis Book Publishing Corporation Limited
Greater London House, Hampstead Road
London NW1 7QX
A BPCC plc company

© 1986 The Festival Press Limited
© text 1986 Richard Cawley
© photographs 1986 Trevor Richards

This book was designed and edited by
The Festival Press Limited
5 Dryden Street, Covent Garden, London WC2E 9NW

British Library Cataloguing in Publication Data
Cawley, Richard
    Not quite vegetarian: exciting recipes
    for our changing lifestyle.
    1. Cookery (Natural foods)
    I. Title
    641.5'637   TX741

ISBN 0-356-12772-9

Printed in Italy

Acknowledgements

The Festival Press Limited and Richard Cawley would like to thank the following people and organisations for their contributions to this book: Ian Hands, styling and cookery assistant; Norma MacMillan, copy editor; Andrew Whittle; The General Trading Company (Mayfair) Limited, 144 Sloane Street, London SW1; David Mellor, 4 Sloane Street, London SW1W 8EE, 26 James Street, London WC2E 8PA, 66 King Street, Manchester M2 4NP.

Front cover: Ribbons of plaice, steamed in leaves with Hot root and fruit salad (pp. 108/9).

Back cover: top right, and then clockwise: Cheese roulade with Waldorf filling; Strawberries in Champagne; Trifle; Salmon three ways; Mushroom-stuffed brioche ring; Turkey breast with confetti vegetable stuffing and Red and green salad (pp. 128-132).

Title page: Ricotta cheese and fresh fruit (p.125).

CONTENTS

The dishes are arranged in menus, planned as balanced meals, kept light and fresh, and presented beautifully. The first menu in each chapter is for party food — at home, as a picnic, or for a barbecue. The remaining menus serve six people, and can be used for dinner parties or absorbed into the everyday repertoire of a healthy family diet.

6 A Taste of Sunshine

Nothing tastes better than the first fruits and vegetables of a season, freshly picked and simply prepared. Modern transportation methods ensure an enormous variety of fresh food all the year round — not just the familiar ones, but new and interesting ingredients from all over the world.

34 More Taste than Money

Special meals can be prepared on a low budget. Fresh ingredients, simply but elegantly prepared, can produce the most sparkling results. Expensive meat and fish need not appear at all, unless in very small amounts as garnishes or a final flourish.

58 Eastern Promise

Oriental and specialist food shops offer fresh, dried and tinned exotic foods for adventurous cooks to recreate and adapt the classic cuisines of the East. Experiment with the new tastes, textures and aromas for a dinner party with a difference.

82 Fast Feasts

The occasional meal of prepacked food need not be hazardous to our health or injurious to our taste buds. Stores now stock a wide range of foods that are additive free. Most of these recipes require very little preparation — either in advance or at the last minute.

102 Thinner Dinners

When the intake of sugars and fats of all kinds needs to be cut and some weight lost, do not despair. Fresh fruit and vegetables, eaten raw wherever possible, will aid gradual and healthy weight reduction with no loss of pleasure either for those that do need to lose weight or for those that don't.

126 Putting on the Style

Spectacular menus for those very special occasions, when nothing but the best will do, incur a little more time, a little more money and a little more effort. These menus call for the most elegant presentation — polished silver, starched linen, candlelight, music and fresh-cut flowers for a truly glamorous occasion.

156 Basic Recipes
159 Index

A TASTE OF SUNSHINE

HAND TO MOUTH PARTY FOODS Party menu for 12 people
Crudités with three dips
Aubergine and sesame dip
Avocado, chilli and yogurt dip
Tomato and anchovy mayonnaise dip
Hard-boiled quails' eggs
Mussels in sour cream on the half shell
Deep-fried smoked oysters in puff pastry
Stuffed mange-touts
Mushroom and grape tartlets

Right: top left, and then clockwise:
Mushroom and grape tartlets; Deep-fried smoked oysters in puff pastry; Crudités with three dips; Stuffed mange-touts; Mussels in sour cream on the half shell; Hard-boiled quails' eggs; pp6-11.

Crudités with three dips

Make a selection – varied in colour, flavour and texture – of crisp salad ingredients, plus raw and cooked vegetables chosen from the following: wedges of iceberg lettuce, chicory [endive] leaves, radishes, spring onions [scallions], cherry tomatoes, fennel slices, strips of red, green and yellow peppers, raw mushrooms, raw cauliflower florets, cucumber sticks, celery sticks, mange-touts [snow peas] and stick or French beans [green beans] (blanched for 2 minutes), cooked asparagus, etc.

To serve, arrange the crudités in attractive baskets, dishes or platters. Serve with the following dips.

Aubergine and sesame dip

Metric	Imperial	USA	
450g	1lb	1lb	aubergines [eggplants], about 2
45ml	3tbsp	3tbsp	lemon juice
60ml	4tbsp	4tbsp	tahini (sesame paste)
2	2	2	garlic cloves, peeled and crushed
10ml	2tsp	2tsp	salt
			freshly ground black pepper
60ml	4tbsp	¼ cup	finely chopped parsley

Oven temperature:
230°C/450°F/Gas Mark 8
Preparation time: 45 minutes
plus cooling and chilling

1 Prick the aubergines [eggplants] with a fork and bake in the oven for about 30 minutes, or until quite soft when squeezed. Leave until cool enough to handle, then split open and scrape out all the flesh.
2 Put the flesh in a blender or food processor with the lemon juice, tahini, garlic, salt and pepper to taste and blend until smooth. Stir in the chopped parsley and spoon into a serving dish. Cover closely.
3 Chill for at least 2 hours before serving, to allow the flavours to develop.

Avocado, chilli and yogurt dip

Metric	Imperial	USA	
2	2	2	large ripe avocados, peeled, stoned and chopped
			juice of ½ large lemon
90ml	6tbsp	6tbsp	plain yogurt
5ml	1tsp	1tsp	chilli powder, or more to taste
			salt

Preparation time: 15 minutes
plus chilling

1 Put all the ingredients into a blender or food processor and blend until smooth. Check the seasoning and spoon into a serving dish. Cover closely.
2 Chill for at least 2 hours before serving, to allow the flavours to develop.

Tomato and anchovy mayonnaise dip

Metric	Imperial	USA	
2	2	2	eggs
50-g	2-oz	2-oz	can anchovy fillets, drained
150ml	¼ pint	⅔ cup	olive oil
150ml	¼ pint	⅔ cup	vegetable oil
			juice of 1 lemon
30ml	2tbsp	2tbsp	concentrated tomato purée [paste]
			freshly ground black pepper
5ml	1tsp	1tsp	sugar
200ml	⅓ pint	1 cup	double [heavy] cream, lightly whipped

1 Place the eggs and anchovies in a blender or food processor and blend for 30 seconds. Mix together the oils and pour into the blender or processor, with the motor running, in a slow steady stream to produce a smooth, thick mayonnaise.

Preparation time: 10 minutes plus chilling

2 Add the lemon juice, tomato purée, pepper to taste and sugar and blend until well mixed. Fold in the whipped cream and spoon into a serving dish. Cover closely.

3 Chill for at least 2 hours before serving, to allow the flavours to develop.
NOTE No salt is necessary as this is provided by the anchovies.

Hard-boiled quails' eggs

	Metric	Imperial	USA
quails' eggs (or more)	48	48	48
sea salt			

1 Place the eggs carefully in a pan of cold water. Bring to the boil and simmer for 3 minutes.

Preparation time: 10-15 minutes

2 Pour off the hot water and immediately cover the eggs with cold water to arrest cooking and stop the yolks from discolouring.

3 To serve, peel some of the eggs, but leave the rest in their shells as they look so decorative. Slice a few peeled eggs in half, to show their yolks and add a splash of colour. Arrange in a bowl or basket or on a plate, and serve with a bowl of salt for guests to dip the eggs in as desired.

Mussels in sour cream on the half shell

	Metric	Imperial	USA
live mussels in shells	2kg	4½lb	4½lb
sour cream or double [heavy] cream	300ml	½ pint	1¼ cups
lemon juice	20ml	4tsp	4tsp
freshly ground black pepper			

1 Scrub the mussels thoroughly in cold water, removing any barnacles with a sharp knife. Rinse and drain. Using a thumb and the blade of a knife, strip away any 'beard' which protrudes from the straight side of the shell. Rinse again under running water.

Preparation time: 1 hour plus soaking

2 Leave the mussels to soak in cold water for at least 1 hour to remove any traces of dirt or sand. Change the water at least three times.

3 Meanwhile, if you are not using sour cream, mix together the cream and lemon juice and leave in a cool place for 30 minutes.

4 Drain the mussels. Any which remain open after being given a sharp tap with a knife handle should be discarded. Open the mussels in two or three batches by placing them in a large heavy-bottomed pan with a tight-fitting lid over a medium heat. It is not necessary to add any liquid to the pan: the mussels will soon release their own liquid. After one or two minutes, uncover the pan and remove any mussels that have opened. Put them in a colander to drain. (Mussels need very little cooking or they become tough.) Continue until all the mussels are opened – any which stubbornly refuse to open should be discarded.

5 Throw away the empty shell from each mussel and leave to cool.

6 Remove each mussel from its half shell, place a 2.5ml/½tsp of the sour cream or acidulated cream mixture in the shell and replace the mussel neatly on top.

7 Arrange all the mussels attractively on a large platter and sprinkle over a few twists of pepper.

Deep-fried smoked oysters in puff pastry

Metric	Imperial	USA	
375g	13oz	13oz	puff pastry, thawed if frozen
4×100-g	4×4-oz	4×4-oz	cans smoked oysters, drained
2	2	2	egg yolks
15ml	1tbsp	1tbsp	milk
			oil for deep frying

Preparation time: 45 minutes
plus chilling

1 Roll out the pastry very thinly (work in small batches) and cut out circles measuring 7cm/2¾ inches in diameter.

2 Place an oyster in the centre of each pastry circle. Dampen the edges of the pastry with a little of the egg yolk and milk mixed together, fold over into a half-moon shape and pinch the edges to seal. Chill for 30 minutes.

3 Heat the oil until a 2.5cm/1 inch cube of bread will turn golden brown in 1 minute.

4 Fry the oyster puffs in small batches, turning frequently, until crisp and golden. Drain on crumpled paper towels and keep warm while the rest are cooked. Serve hot.

Stuffed mange-touts

Metric	Imperial	USA	
275g	10oz	10oz	small mange-touts [snow peas], topped and tailed
225g	8oz	1 cup	cream or other soft cheese, at room temperature, softened

Preparation time: 45 minutes
plus chilling

1 Cook the mange-touts in boiling salted water for 2 minutes. Drain and immediately plunge into cold water to arrest cooking. When cool, drain and pat dry on paper towels.

2 Split open the pods carefully along one side. Open a pod slightly and hold in one hand. With the other hand, neatly spread a little of the cheese along the inside, using a small knife. Close the pod gently, allowing the cheese to show a little.

3 Arrange on a serving dish, cover closely and chill until required.

Mushroom and grape tartlets
(Make at least 12)

	Metric	Imperial	USA
quantity shortcrust [basic pie] pastry (see page 156)	1	1	1

The filling

	Metric	Imperial	USA
butter	75g	3oz	6tbsp
small onion, peeled and very finely chopped	1	1	1
mushrooms, wiped and very finely chopped	450g	1lb	1lb
garlic cloves, peeled and crushed	4	4	4
finely chopped parsley	60ml	4tbsp	¼ cup
salt and freshly ground black pepper			

Garnish

	Metric	Imperial	USA
butter	50g	2oz	4tbsp
tiny white button mushrooms, finely sliced	50g	2oz	½ cup
small green or black grapes, halved and seeded	100g	4oz	1 cup

1 Roll out the pastry very thinly and use to line small buttered and floured fluted tartlet tins. Bake blind in the oven for about 15 minutes or until crisp and golden. Repeat until all pastry is used up. Set aside.

2 To make the filling, melt the butter in a heavy-bottomed saucepan and add the onion. Cook over medium heat until transparent. Add the mushrooms, garlic, parsley, and salt and pepper to taste. Cover and cook over a very low heat for 30 minutes. Remove the lid occasionally and stir the contents of the pan.

3 If the mushrooms have given off a great quantity of liquid, cook uncovered over a fierce heat, stirring constantly, until most of the liquid has evaporated. The mixture should be moist but not sloppy.

4 Fill the cooked pastry cases with the mushroom mixture.

5 For the garnish, cook the sliced mushrooms in the butter over gentle heat until just tender, 2 or 3 minutes. Arrange the mushroom slices and grape halves on top of the mushroom filling.

6 Just before serving, reheat the tartlets in the oven for about 10 minutes, or until warmed through. Do not allow the pastry to become too dark. Serve hot.

Oven temperature: 220°C/425°F/Gas Mark 7; then 180°C/350°F/Gas Mark 4 to reheat
Preparation time: 2 hours

Gnocchi with gorgonzola sauce
Olive-stuffed artichokes in batter
Hot vegetable salad à la Grecque
Amaretti ice cream

Gnocchi with gorgonzola sauce

Metric	Imperial	USA	
			The gnocchi
700g	1½lb	1½lb	red potatoes
1	1	1	egg, beaten
2.5ml	½tsp	½tsp	salt
200g	7oz	1½ cups	flour
			The sauce
25g	1oz	2tbsp	butter
1	1	1	garlic clove. peeled and crushed
225ml	8floz	1 cup	double [heavy] cream
2.5ml	½tsp	½tsp	chopped fresh sage, or 1.25ml/¼tsp dried
			pinch of salt
100g	4oz	4oz	gorgonzola cheese, mashed with a fork
			freshly ground black pepper
			chopped parsley, to garnish

Preparation time: about
1 hour

1 To make the gnocchi, cook the potatoes in their skins in boiling salted water until tender. As soon as they are cool enough to handle, peel the potatoes and mash or pass through a food mill. Do *not* purée in a blender or food processor as they will become gluey.

2 Mix in the egg, then add the salt and work in most of the flour. Do not add too much flour – the dough should remain very soft, almost sticky.

3 Shape the dough into long sausages as thick as your thumb, then cut into 2.5cm/1 inch lengths. Italians make these into the traditional grooved shape with a deft light prod and a flick of an index finger against the prongs of a fork. This leaves the little dumpling slightly hollow on one side and grooved on the other. They taste just as good, however, simply cut into smooth lengths.

4 Bring a large pan of water to the boil and drop in the gnocchi in batches of about 15 at a time. When they rise to the surface, which is quite quickly, allow them to simmer for 10 seconds. As soon as they are done, remove with a slotted spoon to a heated dish and keep warm while you cook the rest of the gnocchi.

5 To make the sauce, melt the butter in a small pan over a medium heat, add the garlic and cook for 1 minute. Add the cream, sage, salt and mashed cheese and bring to the boil, stirring. Allow to simmer gently for 5 minutes, stirring constantly and pressing out any lumps with the back of a wooden spoon, until a smooth rich sauce is achieved. Season with a little black pepper.

6 To serve, toss the gnocchi in the sauce and divide between 6 heated bowls. Sprinkle with parsley.

NOTE Grated Parmesan may be handed separately to sprinkle on top, but I find this is not necessary.

Olive-stuffed artichokes in batter

	Metric	Imperial	USA
black olives, stoned	225g	8oz	1½ cups
can anchovy fillets, drained	50-g	2-oz	2-oz
capers	30ml	2tbsp	2tbsp
freshly ground black pepper			
small artichoke bottoms, drained and patted dry with paper towels	12	12	12
oil for frying			

The sauce			
plain yogurt	300ml	½ pint	1¼ cups
dry English mustard	10ml	2tsp	2tsp
sugar	5ml	1tsp	1tsp

The batter			
flour	175g	6oz	1¼ cups
bicarbonate of soda [baking soda]	10ml	2tsp	2tsp
water	175ml	6floz	¾ cup
vinegar	15ml	1tbsp	1tbsp

1 Combine the olives, anchovies and capers in a blender or food processor and blend until smooth. (Alternatively, use a pestle and mortar.) Add pepper to taste.

2 Divide the mixture between the artichoke bottoms, spooning it into the hollow side and smoothing the top with a knife.

3 Make the sauce by mixing the yogurt with the mustard and sugar. Set aside.

4 To make the batter, mix the flour and soda with the water, beating until

Preparation time: 40 minutes

smooth. Just before using, beat in the vinegar.

5 Heat the oil until a 2.5cm/1 inch cube of bread will turn golden brown in 1 minute.

6 Being careful not to disturb the stuffing, dip each artichoke bottom in the batter, making sure that every bit is covered. Fry in small batches, turning once, until puffed, crisp and golden. Remove with a slotted spoon and drain on paper towels.

7 Serve onto hot plates, spoon over a little sauce and surround with hot vegetable salad à la Grecque (see following recipe).

Left: top: Gnocchi with gorgonzola sauce; **centre:** Olive-stuffed artichokes in batter with hot vegetable salad 'a la Grecque'; **below:** Amaretti ice cream; pp12-16.

Hot vegetable salad à la Grecque

	Metric	Imperial	USA
dry white wine	300ml	½ pint	1¼ cups
water	300ml	½ pint	1¼ cups
olive oil	75ml	5tbsp	5tbsp
juice of 2 lemons			
large bunch of parsley			
dried thyme, or 2.5ml/½tsp fresh if available	1.25ml	¼tsp	¼tsp
fennel seeds	1.25ml	¼tsp	¼tsp
bay leaf	1	1	1
black peppercorns, lightly crushed	2.5ml	½tsp	½tsp
coriander seeds, lightly crushed	2.5ml	½tsp	½tsp
salt	7.5ml	1½tsp	1½tsp
small button mushrooms, wiped clean	225g	8oz	8oz
small green beans, topped and tailed	225g	8oz	8oz
carrots, scraped and cut into small sticks	225g	8oz	8oz
spring onions [scallions], trimmed and cut into small sticks	3	3	3

1 Place the wine, water, oil and lemon juice in a saucepan with all the herbs and spices. Bring to the boil, then cover and simmer for about 30 minutes.

2 Strain through a fine sieve and return the liquid to the pan. Add the vegetables, cover and simmer for 20-30 minutes or until tender.

3 Remove the vegetables with a slotted spoon to a heated serving dish and keep warm. Turn up the heat under the saucepan and boil to reduce the liquid by half.

4 Pour the liquid over the cooked vegetables and toss to coat. Serve immediately, or allow to go cold before serving.

Preparation time: 1-1¼ hours

Amaretti ice cream

Metric	Imperial	USA	
3	3	3	egg yolks
150g	5oz	⅔ cup	sugar
450ml	¾ pint	2 cups	milk
			pinch of salt
2.5ml	½tsp	½tsp	vanilla essence [extract]
225ml	8fl oz	1 cup	single [light] cream
			thinly pared rind of 1 small orange, cut into julienne strips and blanched for 10 minutes
75g	3oz	1 cup	amaretti biscuits [cookies], crushed
			To serve
6	6	6	amaretti biscuits [cookies]
			slices or segments of peeled orange

Preparation time: 40 minutes plus cooling and freezing

1 Beat the egg yolks with the sugar until pale and creamy.

2 Bring the milk to the boil in a small saucepan, then pour in a steady stream on to the egg yolk mixture. Return to the pan and add the salt and vanilla. Cook over a very low heat, stirring constantly, until the custard coats the back of a wooden spoon. Be patient as this could take 20 minutes or so. If the mixture cooks too quickly the eggs will scramble, forming lumps; if this should happen, purée the mixture in a blender or food processer.

3 Allow the custard to cool, then stir in the cream and pour into a shallow freezerproof container. Freeze until beginning to solidify.

4 Remove from the freezer and whisk well with a fork, mashing out any lumps. Freeze again until beginning to solidify, then whisk again. Mix in the strips of orange rind and crushed amaretti biscuits. Return to the freezer and freeze until solid.

5 Remove the ice cream from the freezer to the refrigerator 1 hour before required, to allow it to soften a little.

6 Spoon on to 6 plates or dishes and garnish with whole amaretti biscuits and orange slices or segments.

Egg, lemon and mussel soup

	Metric	Imperial	USA
vegetable stock (see page 157)	900ml	1½ pints	1 quart
egg yolks	4	4	4
juice of 2 lemons			
salt and freshly ground black pepper			
live mussels in shells, scrubbed and cleaned (see page 9)	2kg	4½lb	4½lb
chopped parsley, to garnish			

1 Bring the stock to the boil in a large saucepan. Mix together the egg yolks and lemon juice in a large bowl. Starting with only a cupful at a time, gradually pour the boiling stock on to the egg yolk mixture, whisking constantly.

2 Return the mixture to the pan and whisk gently over a low heat until the soup thickens slightly. Do not allow the temperature to reach boiling or the eggs will scramble. Add salt and pepper to taste. Remove from the heat and keep hot.

3 Open the mussels in a large saucepan (see pages 9/10). As soon as all the mussels have opened, tip them into the soup and mix together gently.

4 Divide between 6 large, hot, soup dishes or bowls and sprinkle with parsley.

Preparation time: 15 minutes

Mediterranean rabbit

Metric	Imperial	USA	
15ml	1tbsp	1tbsp	olive oil
1	1	1	onion, peeled and chopped
400g	14oz	14oz	boneless rabbit, cut into 2.5cm/1 inch cubes
1	1	1	bay leaf
2	2	2	garlic cloves, peeled and crushed
			salt and freshly ground black pepper
5ml	1tsp	1tsp	chopped fresh sage, or 2.5ml/½tsp dried
1	1	1	thin strip orange rind, approximately 2.5×7.5cm/1×3 inches
			juice of 1 orange
120ml	4fl oz	½ cup	white wine
30ml	2tbsp	2tbsp	concentrated tomato purée [paste], dissolved in 150ml/¼ pint [⅔ cup] water
100g	4oz	¾ cup	black olives, stoned
			arrowroot (optional)

Preparation time: about 1¼ hours

1 Heat the oil in a heavy-bottomed pan and cook the onion until pale golden. Add the meat and continue to cook over a medium heat until sealed all over.

2 Add the remaining ingredients, except the arrowroot, cover tightly and leave to simmer over a very low heat for about 1 hour or until the meat is tender.

3 Check for seasoning, and thicken with a little arrowroot dissolved in 15ml/1tbsp water if desired. Serve with vegetable and rice timbales (see following recipe).

Right: top: Vegetable and rice timbale; **centre left:** Egg, lemon and mussel soup; **centre right:** Mediterranean rabbit; **below:** Hearts of cream cheese with soft fruits; pp17-21.

Vegetable and rice timbale

Metric	Imperial	USA	
			fine white breadcrumbs
225g	8oz	8oz	mozzarella cheese, thinly sliced
25g	1oz	2tbsp	cold butter, cut into tiny pieces

The risotto

Metric	Imperial	USA	
25g	1oz	2tbsp	butter
15ml	1tbsp	1tbsp	vegetable oil
1	1	1	small onion, peeled and finely chopped
1	1	1	garlic clove, peeled and crushed
275g	10oz	1⅔ cups	Italian arborio rice
900ml	1½ pints	3¾ cups	vegetable stock (see page 157) or more if needed
50g	2oz	½ cup	Parmesan cheese, freshly grated

The filling

Metric	Imperial	USA	
15ml	1tbsp	1tbsp	olive oil
1	1	1	leek, trimmed and chopped
1	1	1	large carrot, scrubbed and chopped
100g	4oz	1 cup	mushrooms, wiped and sliced
1	1	1	large tomato, skinned and chopped
150ml	¼ pint	⅔ cup	vegetable or chicken stock (see page 156)
150ml	¼ pint	⅔ cup	white wine
			salt and freshly ground black pepper

Oven temperature: 190°C/
375°F/Gas Mark 5
Preparation time: about
2¼ hours plus cooling

1 Heat the butter and oil in a large pan and cook the onion until transparent. Add the garlic and rice and cook, stirring, for 2-3 minutes.
2 Bring the stock to boiling point in another pan and keep warm over a low heat.
3 Ladle just enough hot stock over the rice to cover. Cook over medium heat, stirring occasionally, until all the liquid has been absorbed, then add another ladleful of stock. Never add more stock than will just cover the rice. Continue this process until all the stock has been added and the rice is cooked – 20-25 minutes. The finished risotto should be moist and creamy with a little bite left in the centre of each grain of rice. About 5 minutes before the risotto is cooked, stir in the grated Parmesan.
4 Allow to go completely cold.
5 For the filling, heat the oil and cook the leek, carrot and mushrooms for 2-3 minutes, stirring occasionally. Add the chopped tomato, stock, wine and salt and pepper to taste. Cover and cook for about 15 minutes, or until the carrot is just tender. Leave to go cold, then drain, reserving the liquid.
6 Tip the breadcrumbs into a very well-buttered 1.4 litre/2½ pint

pudding basin [1 ½ quart round deep casserole or steaming mould]. Shake until evenly coated with crumbs. Next line the basin with about three-quarters of the cold risotto. Fill the centre with alternating layers of sliced mozzarella and vegetables, and pour in the reserved vegetable cooking liquid. Carefully cover with the remaining risotto. Sprinkle with more breadcrumbs and dot with the butter.

7 Bake in the oven for 1 hour. The top should be very crisp and brown. Carefully turn out on to a large hot plate and serve.

NOTE Any leftovers are delicious cold.

Hearts of cream cheese with soft fruits

	Metric	Imperial	USA
double [heavy] cream	300ml	½ pint	1 ¼ cups
cream cheese	225g	8oz	1 cup
caster [superfine] sugar	15ml	1 tbsp	1 tbsp
egg whites	2	2	2
soft fruit, such as strawberries, raspberries, frais de bois, etc	450g	1lb	1lb

1 Slowly work the cream into the cheese with the sugar, using a wooden spoon.

2 Beat the egg whites until stiff but not dry, and fold these gently into the cheese mixture.

3 Line 6 perforated heart-shaped moulds with damp muslin or cheese-cloth. (These moulds are specially made for the purpose and are available from kitchen supply shops and department stores.)

4 Spoon the mixture evenly into the moulds and place these on a large plate. Leave in the refrigerator overnight or for several hours to drain and chill.

5 At the last minute, unmould each heart on to a plate and surround with fruit.

Preparation time: 15 minutes plus draining

Salad with warm chicken livers and mustard fruits
Roquefort and cranberry tarts
Wilted garlic spinach
Coffee ice with cream

Far left: Salad with warm chicken livers and mustard fruits; p23.
Left: Roquefort and cranberry tarts with Wilted garlic spinach; p24.

Salad with warm chicken livers and mustard fruits

	Metric	Imperial	USA
an assortment of seasonal salad leaves (as varied and interesting as possible), torn into small pieces			
butter	50g	2oz	4tbsp
garlic clove, peeled and crushed	1	1	1
chicken livers, trimmed and cut into bite-size pieces	450g	1lb	1lb
salt and freshly ground black pepper			
brandy	30ml	2tbsp	2tbsp
lemon juice	30ml	2tbsp	2tbsp
fruit syrup from jar of fruit	45ml	3tbsp	3tbsp
'mostarda di cremona' fruits, cut into small pieces	150g	5oz	1 cup

Preparation time: 20 minutes

1 Arrange the salad leaves in little 'nests' on the centre of 6 large plates. Set aside.

2 Melt the butter in a frying pan, add the garlic, chicken livers and salt and pepper to taste and cook, stirring gently, until the livers are just done – that is, until the blood has stopped running. Add the brandy, warm briefly and set alight with a match. When the flames die down, add the lemon juice and syrup and continue cooking, stirring, just until the sauce is hot.

3 Divide the hot livers between the 6 plates, scattering them on to the leaves with the fruit pieces, pour over the hot sauce and serve at once.

Roquefort and cranberry tarts

Metric	Imperial	USA	
1	1	1	quantity shortcrust [basic pie] pastry (see page 156)
75g	3oz	¾ cup	fresh cranberries
4	4	4	eggs
300ml	½ pint	1¼ cups	double [heavy] cream
100g	4oz	4oz	Roquefort cheese, mashed with a fork
			freshly ground black pepper

Oven temperature: 220°C/ 425°F/Gas Mark 7.
Preparation time: 50 minutes

1 Roll out the pastry and use to line 6 10cm/4 inch loose-bottomed tartlet tins. Divide the cranberries between these.

2 Whisk the eggs lightly with the cream. Mix in the cheese and season with a few twists of pepper.

3 Pour into the pastry cases and bake in the oven for about 30 minutes or until puffed and golden.

4 Serve immediately on hot plates, surrounded by wilted garlic spinach (see following recipe).

NOTE If cranberries are out of season these tarts are still delicious without them.

Wilted garlic spinach

Metric	Imperial	USA	
100g	4oz	8tbsp	butter
3	3	3	garlic cloves, peeled and crushed
1.5kg	3lb	3lb	young spinach, washed and dried
			salt and freshly ground black pepper

Preparation time: 5 minutes

1 Melt the butter in a large saucepan, add the garlic and cook over medium heat for 1 minute.

2 Add the spinach and salt and pepper to taste. Cover the pan and cook, shaking the pan occasionally, just until the spinach is wilted and hot. Serve immediately.

Coffee ice with cream

	Metric	Imperial	USA
sugar	225g	8oz	1 cup
water	300ml	½ pint	1¼ cups
strong freshly made black coffee	900ml	1½ pints	3¾ cups
ground cinnamon	2.5ml	½tsp	½tsp
whipped cream, to serve			

1 Put the sugar and water in a small pan. Bring to the boil and simmer for 5 minutes.
2 Stir in the coffee and cinnamon and allow to cool.
3 Pour into a freezerproof container and freeze undisturbed for at least 4 hours.
4 Remove to the refrigerator 1 hour before serving.
5 To serve, spoon into chilled glasses or bowls and top with cream.

Preparation time: 15 minutes plus cooling and freezing

Cockles in 'snail butter'
Green risotto
Salad with hot chèvre
Mango and grape nests in kiwi pools

Cockles in 'snail butter'

	Metric	Imperial	USA
butter	100g	4oz	8tbsp
garlic cloves, peeled and crushed	3	3	3
chopped parsley	30ml	2tbsp	2tbsp
salt and freshly ground black pepper			
cooked shelled cockles or small clams (not in brine or vinegar)	350g	12oz	12oz

1 Melt the butter in a small pan over a low heat. Add the garlic, parsley and salt and pepper to taste and cook gently for 2 minutes. Do not let the butter colour.
2 Divide the cockles between 6 small ovenproof dishes or ramekins. Pour over the garlic butter. Cover with foil and place on a baking sheet.
3 Bake in the oven for 10-15 minutes or just until the cockles are hot. Do not overcook as the cockles will toughen.
4 Serve immediately, with bread to mop up the garlic butter.

Oven temperature: 220°C/ 425°F/Gas Mark 7
Preparation time: 30 minutes

Left: Cockles in 'snail butter'; p25.

Below: Mango and grape nests in kiwi pools; p29.

Green risotto

Metric	Imperial	USA	
2	2	2	celery stalks, thinly sliced
4	4	4	large spring onions [scallions], chopped with as much of the green as possible
100g	4oz	4oz	green beans, trimmed and cut into 2.5cm/1 inch pieces
175g	6oz	6oz	small broccoli spears, tops cut into florets and stems sliced
100g	4oz	1 cup	peas, thawed if frozen
100g	4oz	1 cup	green peppers, seeded and chopped
60ml	4tbsp	¼ cup	finely chopped parsley
			salt and freshly ground black pepper

The risotto

Metric	Imperial	USA	
25g	1oz	2tbsp	butter
15ml	1tbsp	1tbsp	vegetable oil
1	1	1	large onion, peeled and chopped
2	2	2	garlic cloves, peeled and crushed
425g	15oz	2½ cups	Italian arborio rice
1.8 litres	3 pints	7½ cups	chicken or vegetable stock (see page 156)
50g	2oz	½ cup	Parmesan cheese, freshly grated

Preparation time: 45 minutes

1 Make the risotto, following steps 1-3 of the recipe for vegetable and rice timbale on page 20.

2 Meanwhile, steam the celery, onions, beans, broccoli, peas and green pepper together until just tender.

3 Stir the steamed vegetables and parsley into the basic risotto and add salt and pepper to taste. Divide between 6 heated soup dishes or plates and serve.

NOTE Other fresh green herbs can be added as available.

Salad with hot chèvre

Metric	Imperial	USA	
			an assortment of fresh salad leaves as available (as varied and interesting as possible), shredded
1	1	1	quantity vinaigrette dressing (see page 158)
6	6	6	round slices of goat's cheese, about 25g/1oz each
6	6	6	round slices of wholemeal [wholewheat] bread same size as cheese, toasted

Preparation time: 15 minutes

1 Toss the shredded leaves in the vinaigrette and arrange as small 'nests' in the centre of 6 very large plates.

2 Place the rounds of cheese on the toast and put under a preheated hot grill [broiler] until the cheese is bubbling and brown.

3 Quickly place a circle of toast and cheese in the centre of each salad 'nest'. Serve immediately.

Mango and grape nests in kiwi pools

	Metric	Imperial	USA
ripe kiwi fruit, peeled and chopped	4	4	4
juice of 1 lemon			
water	30ml	2tbsp	2tbsp
sugar	30ml	2tbsp	2tbsp
ripe mangos, peeled and stoned	3	3	3
seedless green grapes, halved and chilled	350g	12oz	12oz

1 Put the kiwi fruit, lemon juice, water and sugar in a blender or food processor and blend until smooth.
2 Cut the mango flesh into small slivers about 4cm/1 ½ inches long. Chill.
3 To serve, divide the mango slivers into six portions and form into circular nests in the centre of 6 chilled plates. Fill with grape halves and surround with the kiwi sauce.

Preparation time: 20 minutes plus chilling

*Terrine of feta cheese and olives
with taramasalata sauce
Fresh pasta with mushrooms and broad beans
in herbed garlic butter
Seafood platter
Chilled fresh figs with Campari sabayon sauce*

Terrine of feta cheese and olives with taramasalata sauce

	Metric	Imperial	USA
feta cheese	175g	6oz	6oz
chicken or vegetable stock (see page 156)	300ml	½ pint	1 ¼ cups
unflavoured gelatine	1 sachet	1 sachet	1 env.
double [heavy] cream, lightly whipped	150ml	¼ pint	⅔ cup
egg white, beaten until stiff but not dry	1	1	1
black olives, stoned and coarsely chopped	100g	4oz	⅔ cup
taramasalata, bought ready made	150ml	¼ pint	⅔ cup
plain yogurt	60ml	4tbsp	¼ cup

1 Put the cheese in a blender or food processor with half the stock and blend until smooth. Dissolve the gelatine in the rest of the stock over a low heat. Add the gelatine mixture to the cheese mixture and blend for 2-3 seconds. Pour into a bowl.

Preparation time: 20 minutes plus chilling

Above: Terrine of feta cheese and olives with taramasalata sauce; p29.
Right: Fresh pasta with mushrooms and broad beans in herbed garlic butter; p32.
Far right: Seafood platter; p33.

2 Fold in the cream and then the egg white. Pour half this mixture into a wet 900ml/1½ pint [1 quart] terrine or loaf tin and chill until almost set. If the mixture in the bowl should begin to set, place it over another bowl filled with warm water.

3 Press the chopped olives all over the surface of the almost set mixture in the terrine and chill until completely set.

4 Pour on the rest of the cheese mixture and chill for at least 3 hours.

5 Make the sauce by simply mixing the taramasalata with the yogurt.

6 To serve, run a knife around the terrine to loosen it, dip the mould in boiling water for 1-2 seconds, no longer, then turn out onto a plate. Cut into thick slices. Place a slice on each plate and spoon a little sauce next to it. NOTE This is delicious served with pitta bread.

Fresh pasta with mushrooms and beans in herbed garlic butter

Metric	Imperial	USA	
175g	6oz	12 tbsp	butter
175g	6oz	1½ cups	mushrooms, wiped and sliced
3	3	3	garlic cloves, peeled and crushed
45ml	3tbsp	3tbsp	chopped mixed fresh herbs such as parsley, basil and chives
450g	1lb	1lb	shelled broad or lima beans, thawed if frozen
500g	18oz	18oz	fresh pasta, half green and half white
			salt and freshly ground black pepper

Preparation time: 15 minutes

1 Melt the butter in a small saucepan, add the mushrooms, garlic and half the herbs and cook, stirring occasionally, for 5 minutes.

2 Meanwhile, steam or boil the beans until tender, and cook the pasta in plenty of boiling salted water for 3-4 minutes or until just tender. Drain.

3 Add the beans and the rest of the herbs to the mushrooms. Add salt and pepper to taste. Continue to cook, stirring, for 2-3 seconds.

4 Divide the cooked pasta between 6 heated plates or dishes and spoon over the vegetables, making sure that each plate gets an equal share of the butter from the pan.

Seafood platter

	Metric	Imperial	USA
lettuce, shredded	1	1	1
a selection of the following fish (quantity and variety to suit appetites and pocket): smoked salmon, smoked trout, smoked mackerel, smoked mussels, smoked oysters, smoked clams, cooked prawns and shrimps (with and without shells), cooked cockles, or clams, cooked mussels, cooked winkles and whelks, dressed crab, cooked crab claws, oysters etc.			
lemon wedges	12	12	12
horseradish sauce, bought ready prepared			
quantity of mayonnaise (see page 158)	1	1	1
freshly ground black pepper			

Cover 6 chilled plates with shredded lettuce. Arrange the assorted fish and shellfish over this and garnish with lemon wedges. Hand horseradish sauce, mayonnaise and a peppermill separately.
NOTE Don't forget nutcrackers, if serving crab claws, lobster etc, and pins if serving winkles in shells.

Preparation time: 20 minutes

Chilled fresh figs with Campari sabayon sauce

	Metric	Imperial	USA
fresh ripe figs, or more, chilled	18	18	18
water	300ml	1/2 pint	1 1/4 cups
sugar	100g	4oz	1/2 cup
eggs	3	3	3
Campari	45-60ml	3-4tbsp	3-4tbsp

1 Make a cross-shaped cut in the top of each fig, cutting three-quarters of the way down to the base. Open out each fruit slightly to show the pink insides. Place the figs on 6 plates and set aside.
2 Boil the water with the sugar in a saucepan until reduced by half.
3 Place the eggs in a bowl suspended over a pan of simmering water. The bottom of the bowl must on no account come in contact with the water. Whisking constantly, pour on the hot sugar syrup in a thin steady stream. Continue to whisk until the sauce thickens enough to coat the back of a spoon. This will take about 5 minutes. Still whisking, add the Campari.
4 Pour the warm sauce next to the figs and serve.

Preparation time: 25-30 minutes

MORE TASTE THAN MONEY

SOUP AND SALAD SUPPER Party menu for 12 people
Stilton and onion soup
Beetroot and orange soup
Seafood and sweetcorn chowder
Pease pottage hot
Herb bread
Olive and garlic bread
Cabbage, carrot and caper salad
Spinach salad with hot garlic croûtons
Real blancmange
Posh spotted dick
Custard sauce

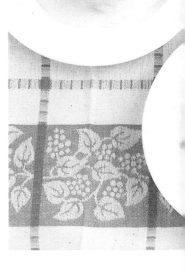

Right: top left, and then clockwise: Real blancmange; Beetroot and orange soup; Stilton and onion soup; Cabbage, carrot and caper salad; Seafood and sweetcorn chowder; Spinach salad with hot garlic croûtons; Posh spotted dick and Custard sauce; **centre:** Pease pottage hot; pp36-40.

Stilton and onion soup

Metric	Imperial	USA	
30ml	2tbsp	2tbsp	vegetable oil
2	2	2	large onions, peeled and chopped
900ml	1½ pints	3¾ cups	chicken or vegetable stock (see page 156)
1	1	1	small onion, peeled and cut into rings
15ml	1tbsp	1tbsp	olive oil
225g	8oz	8oz	Stilton cheese, chopped
10ml	2tsp	2tsp	dry English mustard
600ml	1 pint	2½ cups	milk
			salt and freshly ground black pepper
90ml	6tbsp	6tbsp	single [light] cream

Preparation time: 30 minutes

1 Heat the vegetable oil in a large pan and cook the chopped onions until transparent. Add the stock and simmer for 10 minutes.

2 Meanwhile, fry the onion rings in the olive oil until brown. Drain and keep hot.

3 Pour the soup into a blender or food processor and add the cheese, mustard and milk. Blend until smooth.

4 Return to the pan, reheat and season to taste with salt and pepper. Pour into heated bowls and garnish with the fried onion rings and cream.

Beetroot and orange soup

Metric	Imperial	USA	
1.5 litres	2½ pints	6¼ cups	chicken or vegetable stock (see page 156)
275g	10oz	2 cups	cooked beetroot [beets], peeled and finely diced
3	3	3	spring onions [scallions], trimmed and chopped including the green parts
5ml	1tsp	1tsp	caraway seeds
			rind of 1 small orange, cut into julienne strips
			juice of 4 oranges
			salt and freshly ground black pepper
			orange slices, to garnish

Preparation time: 30 minutes

1 Place all the ingredients in a large pan and bring to the boil. Simmer for 20 minutes.

2 Check the seasoning, and serve with slices of orange floating in the soup as a garnish.

Seafood and sweetcorn chowder

	Metric	Imperial	USA
butter	50g	2oz	4tbsp
onion, peeled and chopped	1	1	1
fennel seed	1.25ml	¼tsp	¼tsp
can sweetcorn kernels, drained	350-g	12-oz	12-oz
chicken or vegetable stock (see page 156)	900ml	1½ pints	3½ cups
salt and freshly ground black pepper			
milk	900ml	1½ pints	3½ cups
shelled cooked prawns [shrimp], thawed if frozen	100g	4oz	4oz
cockles or clams, cooked and shelled	100g	4oz	4oz
skinned cod fillet, cut into 1cm/½ inch cubes	225g	8oz	8oz

Preparation time: 30 minutes

1 Melt the butter in a large pan over a medium heat and cook the onion until transparent. Add the fennel seed, sweetcorn, stock and salt and pepper to taste. Simmer for 15 minutes.
2 Blend the soup in a blender or food processor until coarse-fine: there should still be some bits of corn visible in the soup.
3 Return to the pan. Add the milk and bring to the boil. Turn down the heat to low, add the seafood and simmer only 2 minutes. Serve hot.
NOTE The soup can be made earlier in the day, then reheated, and the fish added just before serving.

Pease pottage hot

	Metric	Imperial	USA
butter	50g	2oz	4tbsp
olive oil	15ml	1tbsp	1tbsp
large onion, peeled and chopped	1	1	1
garlic cloves, peeled and crushed	2	2	2
chopped fresh sage, or 1.25ml/¼tsp dried	2.5ml	½tsp	½tsp
chicken or vegetable stock (see page 156)	1.5 litres	2½ pints	6¼ cups
dried peas, soaked according to instructions on the packed and drained	250g	9oz	1¼ cups
salt and freshly ground black pepper			
chopped parsley, to garnish			

Preparation time: 45 minutes

1 Heat the butter and oil in a large saucepan and cook the onion until transparent. Add the remaining ingredients and simmer for 20-30 minutes or until the peas are mushy.
2 Sprinkle over parsley and serve.

Herb bread

Metric	Imperial	USA	
900g	2lb	6½ cups	strong white [bread] flour
15ml	1tbsp	1tbsp	salt
1	1	2	sachet easy-blend dried yeast [packages active dry yeast]
40g	1½oz	3tbsp	butter, cut into small pieces
60ml	4tbsp	¼ cup	chopped parsley
30ml	2tbsp	2tbsp	chopped mixed fresh herbs, or 15ml/1tbsp dried herbs
600ml	1 pint	2½ cups	hand-hot water

Oven temperature: 230°C/
450°F/Gas Mark 8
Preparation time: 1 hour plus
rising

1 Put the flour in a large bowl with the salt and yeast. Rub in the butter. Mix in the herbs, then add the water according to the yeast instructions. Add a little more water if necessary to make a dough.
2 Turn on to a floured board and knead for 10 minutes.
3 Divide the dough into two equal pieces and shape each into a flattish round. Place these on floured baking sheets and leave somewhere warm to rise until doubled in size, 1-2 hours.
4 Bake in the oven for about 30 minutes or until cooked.

Olive and garlic bread

Metric	Imperial	USA	
900g	2lb	6½ cups	wholemeal [wholewheat] flour
10ml	2tsp	2tsp	salt
1	1	2	sachet easy-blend dried yeast [packages active dry yeast]
15ml	1tbsp	1tbsp	olive oil
600ml	1 pint	2½ cups	hand-hot water
3	3	3	garlic cloves, peeled and crushed
100g	4oz	1 cup	green or black olives, stoned and finely chopped

Oven temperature: 230°C/
450°F/Gas Mark 8
Preparation time: 1 hour plus
rising

1 Put the flour in a large mixing bowl with the salt and yeast. Mix in the oil, water and garlic, adding a little more water if necessary to make a dough. Turn on to a well floured work surface and knead for 10 minutes. Sprinkle over the olive pieces and knead them into the dough until they are evenly dispersed.
2 Divide the dough into two large flattish rounds and place these on floured baking sheets. Leave to rise somewhere warm until doubled in size.
3 Bake in the oven for about 30 minutes or until cooked.

Cabbage, carrot and caper salad

	Metric	Imperial	USA
white cabbage, finely shredded	450g	1lb	1lb
carrots, scrubbed and grated	450g	1lb	1lb
capers, roughly chopped	30ml	2tbsp	2tbsp
quantities vinaigrette dressing (see page 158)	2	2	2

Mix the cabbage and carrots with the capers in a large bowl. At the last minute, toss with the vinaigrette dressing.

Preparation time: 10 minutes

Spinach salad with hot garlic croûtons

	Metric	Imperial	USA
butter	50g	2oz	4tbsp
olive oil	30ml	2tbsp	2tbsp
garlic cloves, peeled and crushed	4	4	4
slices white bread, cut into 0.5cm/¼ inch cubes	6	6	6
very young fresh spinach leaves, washed and dried	450g	1lb	1lb
quantities vinaigrette dressing (see page 158)	2	2	2

1. Heat the butter and oil with the garlic in a large frying pan or wok. Add the cubes of bread in batches and fry until crisp. Drain on paper towels and keep warm.

Preparation time: 15 minutes

2 In a large bowl, toss the spinach in the vinaigrette.
3 Sprinkle the hot croûtons over the spinach and serve.
NOTE This salad should be dressed at the last minute or the spinach will go soggy.

Real blancmange

	Metric	Imperial	USA
ground almonds	225g	8oz	1½ cups
water	150ml	¼ pint	⅔ cup
milk	225ml	8fl oz	1 cup
unflavoured gelatine	2 sachets	2 sachets	2 env.
icing [confectioners'] sugar	350g	12oz	4 cups
single [light] cream	600ml	1 pint	2½ cups

1 Soak the almonds in the water for 30 minutes. Strain through muslin or cheesecloth into a measuring jug, squeezing hard to extract every drop of 'almond milk'. Make up to 600ml/1 pint [2½ cups] with milk and pour into a saucepan.

Preparation time: 45 minutes plus cooling and chilling

2 Bring to almost boiling over a low heat. Sprinkle on the gelatine, then continue to stir over a low heat until the gelatine is dissolved.

3 Sift the sugar into a bowl. Pour the gelatine mixture into the bowl through a fine sieve, pressing through any lumps with the back of a wooden spoon. Stir well and leave to cool.

4 Stir in the cream and pour into a very lightly oiled 1.2 litre/2 pint [5 cup] mould (or 12 small moulds). Chill until set. Turn out when required.

NOTE This blancmange is delicious served on its own, but is excellent with a sauce made from puréed fruit.

Posh spotted dick

Metric	Imperial	USA	
450g	1lb	3¼ cups	self-raising flour
			large pinch of salt
225g	8oz	½lb	butter
100g	4oz	½ cup	caster [granulated] sugar
275g	10oz	1⅔ cups	raisins, soaked in a covered bowl in 120ml/8tbsp dark rum for 12 hours
150ml	¼ pint	⅔-1 cup	water

Preparation time: 1¾ hours

1 Place the flour and salt in a bowl and rub in the butter. Stir in the sugar and soaked raisins. Mix in the water to make a soft dough.

2 Divide the dough into two equal portions. Turn on to a floured work surface and form each portion into a roll.

3 Wrap each roll loosely but securely in buttered foil, allowing room for the pudding to rise.

4 Place in a steamer and steam for 1½ hours.

5 Slice and serve hot with custard sauce (see following recipe).

Custard sauce

Metric	Imperial	USA	
1.2 litres	2 pints	5 cups	milk
4	4	4	egg yolks
30ml	2tbsp	2tbsp	cornflour [cornstarch]
30ml	2tbsp	2tbsp	sugar
5ml	1tsp	1tsp	vanilla essence [extract]

Preparation time: 10-15 minutes

1 Bring the milk almost to boiling point in a saucepan. While this is heating, whisk the egg yolks with the cornflour, sugar and vanilla until pale. When the milk is almost boiling, pour it in a steady stream on to the egg mixture, whisking all the time.

2 Strain through a sieve back into the saucepan and cook over the lowest possible heat until thickened. This custard will not go lumpy if stirred all the time it is cooking.

Herb sausages in lettuce skins
with fresh tomato sauce
Leek tarts topped with Parmesan soufflé
and green vegetables
Fried citrus fruit in crumbs with apricot sauce

Herb sausages in lettuce skins with fresh tomato sauce

	Metric	Imperial	USA
several large lettuce leaves, preferable Webb's Wonder or iceberg			
hard-boiled eggs, finely chopped	2	2	2
fresh wholemeal [wholewheat] breadcrumbs	100g	4oz	2 cups
chopped parsley	15ml	1tbsp	1tbsp
chopped chives, or green part of spring onion [scallion]	7.5ml	½tbsp	½tbsp
chopped fresh basil, tarragon or other herb	7.5ml	½tbsp	½tbsp
egg, beaten	1	1	1
salt and freshly ground black pepper			

The sauce			
olive oil	15ml	1tbsp	1tbsp
small onion, peeled and chopped	1	1	1
garlic clove, peeled and crushed	1	1	1
ripe tomatoes	450g	1lb	1lb
chopped fresh basil, or pinch of dried oregano	7.5ml	½tbsp	½tbsp
sugar	5ml	1tsp	1tsp
salt and freshly ground black pepper			
water	120ml	4floz	½ cup

1 Blanch the lettuce leaves in a large pan of boiling water for 1-2 minutes or until they just begin to wilt. Refresh in cold water and pat dry on clean towels or paper towels. Cut 18 8.5cm/3½-inch squares from the lettuce leaves to form the sausage 'skins'.

2 Mix the chopped egg with the breadcrumbs, herbs and beaten egg and season generously with salt and pepper. Spoon a little of this stuffing along the centre of each lettuce square; practice will soon show exactly how much. Fold in the ends and then the sides to make a neat oblong parcel. Arrange these parcels, seam side down, on an oiled plate. Steam over boiling water for 20 minutes.

3 Meanwhile, make the sauce. Heat the oil in a small pan and cook the

Preparation time: 45 minutes

onion until transparent. Add the garlic, tomatoes, basil, sugar and salt and pepper to taste. Continue to cook, stirring occasionally, for 5 minutes. Add the water and simmer for 5 more minutes.

4 Pour the sauce into a blender or food processor and blend until smooth. Pour the sauce back into the pan through a wire sieve, pressing it through with the back of a wooden spoon. Discard the debris left in the sieve and reheat the sauce.

5 To serve, pour a little of the sauce on to 6 heated plates and arrange 3 sausages on top.

Below: Herb sausages in lettuce skins with fresh tomato sauce; p41.

Above: Leek tarts topped with Parmesan soufflé and green vegetables, p43.
Above right: Fried citrus fruit with apricot sauce; p44.

Leek tarts topped with Parmesan soufflé and green vegetables

	Metric	Imperial	USA
leeks, trimmed and cut into thin rounds	350g	12oz	12oz
butter	50g	2oz	4tbsp
salt and freshly ground black pepper			
tartlet cases, baked blind	6	6	6
eggs, separated	2	2	2
double [heavy] cream	30ml	2tbsp	2tbsp
Parmesan cheese, freshly grated	25g	1oz	¼ cup
dry English mustard	3.75ml	¾tsp	¾tsp
a selection of fresh seasonal green vegetables			
melted butter			

1 In a small saucepan, stew the leeks in the butter over a low heat, covered, for 10 minutes. Season to taste with salt and pepper. Allow to cool, then divide between the pastry cases.
2 Mix the egg yolks with the cream, Parmesan and mustard. Whisk the egg whites until stiff. Stir about 15ml/1tbsp into the cheese mixture, then fold in the remainder. Quickly spoon this over the leeks.
3 Bake the tarts in the oven for 15 minutes or until the filling is puffed and golden.

Oven temperature: 220°C/425°F/Gas Mark 7
Preparation time: about 1 hour

4 Meanwhile, steam or boil the vegetables until just tender. Season to taste and toss in melted butter.

5 To serve, place a tart in the centre of each of 6 large heated plates and surround with vegetables. Serve immediately.

Fried citrus fruit in crumbs with apricot sauce

Metric	Imperial	USA	
3	3	3	large oranges
3	3	3	grapefruits
100g	4oz	¾ cup	flour
2	2	2	eggs, beaten
225g	8oz	4 cups	fresh white breadcrumbs
50g	2oz	4tbsp	butter
60ml	4tbsp	4tbsp	vegetable oil

			The sauce
100g	4oz	1 cup	dried apricots, soaked overnight in 300ml/½ pint [1¼ cups] water
			juice of 1 grapefruit
15ml	1tbsp	1tbsp	sugar

Preparation time: 45 minutes plus soaking

1 First make the sauce. Put the apricots and their soaking water, the grapefruit juice and sugar in a saucepan and simmer gently for about 15 minutes or until the fruit is really soft. Purée in a blender or food processor and return to the pan. Set aside.

2 Peel the oranges and grapefruits and cut away the flesh between the dividing membranes into segments. Dip each segment first in flour, then in beaten egg and then in breadcrumbs, shaking off the excess at each stage.

3 Heat the butter and oil in a frying pan and fry the fruit in batches over a medium heat until golden brown, turning once. Drain on crumpled paper towels and keep warm in a low oven until all the segments have been cooked.

4 To serve, reheat the sauce if necessary, and pour a little into the centre of 6 small hot plates. Arrange some fruit segments in a semi-circle to one side of this. Serve immediately.

NOTE The fruit can be sprinkled with sugar if more sweetness is desired.

Parsley custards
Apple and chive sauce
Deep-fried stuffed mange-touts
Purée of root vegetables
Tomatoes in virgin olive oil
Baked apple timbales with cider sabayon sauce

Parsley custards

	Metric	Imperial	USA
eggs	4	4	4
egg yolks	2	2	2
single [light] cream	300ml	½ pint	1¼ cups
milk	300ml	½ pint	1¼ cups
chopped parsley	45ml	3tbsp	3tbsp
salt and freshly ground black pepper			

1 Mix the whole eggs with the yolks in a bowl.
2 Heat the cream and milk to almost boiling, then pour in a steady stream on to the eggs, stirring rapidly all the time. Strain the mixture into a jug, stir in the parsley and season to taste with salt and pepper.
3 Pour into 6 dampened ramekin or other ovenproof dishes. Cover each with a small circle of buttered foil.
4 Cook in a bain-marie in the oven for about 45 minutes or until a knife inserted into the custard comes out clean. Remove from the bain-marie and leave to cool for 5 minutes before turning out.
5 To serve, run a knife around the outside of each custard, then turn out on to the centre of hot plates. Surround with a pool of apple and chive sauce (see following recipe) and serve.

Oven temperature: 150°C/ 300°F/Gas Mark 2
Preparation time: 1 hour

Apple and chive sauce

	Metric	Imperial	USA
large cooking apples, peeled, cored and sliced	4	4	4
white wine	15ml	1tbsp	1tbsp
lemon juice	15ml	1tbsp	1tbsp
sugar	7.5ml	½tbsp	½tbsp
butter	25g	1oz	2tbsp
chopped chives	25g	2tbsp	2tbsp

Preparation time: 20 minutes

Far right: Deep-fried stuffed mange-touts with Purée of root vegetables and Tomatoes in virgin olive oil; pp46-48.

1 Place all the ingredients except the chives in a small saucepan. Cover and cook over a very low heat, shaking the pan occasionally, for 8-10 minutes or until the apple is soft.

2 Mash or purée in a blender or food processor until creamy, then stir in the chopped chives. Serve warm or at room temperature.

NOTE If chives are not available, use the green part of spring onions [scallions] instead.

Deep-fried stuffed mange-touts

Metric	Imperial	USA	
175g	6oz	6oz	cream cheese
3	3	3	spring onions [scallions], trimmed and finely chopped
45ml	3tbsp	3tbsp	chopped parsley
			salt and freshly ground black pepper
24	24	24	mange-touts [snow peas], topped and tailed and slit open along straight side
			double quantity of batter (see page 13)
			oil for frying

Preparation time: 30 minutes

1 Mix the cream cheese with the onion and parsley and season to taste with salt and pepper.

2 Stuff the mange-touts with this mixture and press the openings closed.

3 Dip in the batter, making sure they are coated all over, then deep fry in hot oil in small batches until puffed, crisp and golden. Drain on crumpled paper towels.

4 Serve on hot plates accompanied by purée of root vegetables and tomatoes in virgin olive oil (see next recipes).

Purée of root vegetables

Metric	Imperial	USA	
450g	1lb	1lb	parsnips, peeled and cut into pieces
450g	1lb	1lb	swede [rutabaga], peeled and cut into pieces
450g	1lb	1lb	carrots, peeled and sliced
50g	2oz	4tbsp	butter
			freshly grated nutmeg
			salt and freshly ground black pepper

Preparation time: 25 minutes

Steam all the vegetables until tender, then mash or purée in a blender or food processor with the butter. Season with nutmeg, salt and pepper to taste and serve hot.

Tomatoes in virgin olive oil

Metric	Imperial	USA	
45ml	3tbsp	3tbsp	virgin olive oil
15ml	1tbsp	1tbsp	lemon juice
2.5ml	½tsp	½tsp	sugar
			salt and freshly ground black pepper
700g	1½lb	1½lb	tomatoes, skinned, seeded and finely diced
30ml	2tbsp	2tbsp	chopped fresh basil

Preparation time: 15 minutes plus marinating

1 Mix the oil with the lemon juice, sugar and salt and pepper to taste in a bowl. Add the diced tomatoes and mix well together. Cover closely and leave to marinate for at least 2 hours.
2 Just before serving, stir in the chopped basil.
NOTE If fresh basil is not available, substitute parsley, tarragon or chives. On no account use dried herbs of any variety.

Baked apple timbales with cider sabayon sauce

Metric	Imperial	USA	
			butter for greasing
100g	4oz	½ cup	sugar
700g	1½lb	1½lb	cooking apples, peeled, cored and very thinly sliced
			The sauce
2	2	2	egg yolks
25g	1oz	2tbsp	caster [superfine] sugar
150ml	¼ pint	⅔ cup	cider [hard cider]

Oven temperature: 220°C/ 425°F/Gas Mark 7
Preparation time: 40-50 minutes

1 Generously butter 6 ramekins. Put a little sugar in each and shake to coat, tipping out the excess.
2 Neatly fill each ramekin with apple slices, sprinkling each layer with a little sugar. The apples should be packed very tightly and should be heaped a little above the edge of the dish as they shrink when cooked.
3 Cover each pot tightly with a circle of buttered foil. Place on a baking sheet and bake in the oven for 20-30 minutes or until the apples are soft.
4 Meanwhile, make the sauce. Put the egg yolks and sugar in a bowl over boiling water and whisk over a gentle heat until the mixture starts to foam. Add the cider a little at a time, whisking continuously. Keep the sauce warm over hot water; do not allow it to get any hotter.
5 To serve, run a knife around the inside of each pot and turn the apple timbales out on to 6 hot plates. Surround with the sauce.

Filo pastry parcels with cheese and watercress filling
Green pasta rolls with smoked fish filling
and fennel cream sauce
Salad of hot fruit

Filo pastry parcels with cheese and watercress filling

	Metric	Imperial	USA
milk, warmed to blood heat	1.2 litres	2 pints	5 cups
lemon juice	120ml	4fl oz	½ cup
spring onions [scallions], finely chopped	4	4	4
garlic cloves, peeled and crushed	2	2	2
salt and freshly ground black pepper			
bunches of watercress, washed and picked over	2	2	2
sheets of filo pastry, each cut in half widthways	9	9	9
flour mixed to a paste with a little water	30ml	2tbsp	2tbsp
oil for frying			

1 Put the milk in a bowl and stir in the lemon juice. Leave for 30 minutes; it will separate into curds and whey.

2 Pour into a square of clean muslin or cheesecloth. Bring together the four corners, tie together and hang over the sink or from a washing line to drain for 2 hours.

3 Mash the resulting cheese and mix with the onions, garlic and salt and pepper to taste. Finely chop half of one of the bunches of watercress and mix this into the cheese mixture. Divide into 18 equal portions.

4 Place a portion of cheese on the end of each rectangle of pastry and roll up, tucking in the sides, to make 18 small rectangular parcels, each measuring about 4×7.5cm/$1\frac{1}{2} \times 3$ inches. Seal each parcel with a little flour and water paste.

5 Deep fry the parcels in hot oil in small batches, turning once, until golden brown. Drain on paper towels.

6 Arrange attractively on 6 plates, surround with the remaining watercress and serve hot.

NOTE When using filo pastry, work quickly and keep the unused pastry under a damp towel, otherwise the pastry will quickly become hard and crack when handled.

Preparation time: 1¼ hours plus draining

Left: top: *Salad of hot fruit;* **centre:** *Filo pastry parcels with cheese and watercress filling;* **below:** *Green pasta rolls with smoked fish filling and fennel cream sauce; pp49-52.*

Green pasta rolls with smoked fish filling and fennel cream sauce

	Metric	Imperial	USA
sheets of dried green lasagne, each measuring 7.5×18cm/3×7 inches	6	6	6
butter	25g	1oz	2tbsp
small onion, peeled and chopped	½	½	½
cream cheese	50g	2oz	2oz
smoked cod or haddock fillets, skinned and cut in chunks	225g	8oz	8oz
lemon juice	10ml	2tsp	2tsp
turmeric	2.5ml	½tsp	½tsp
egg	1	1	1
salt and freshly ground black pepper			

The sauce			
butter	50g	2oz	4tbsp
fennel bulb, outer leaves removed and finely chopped	1	1	1
single [light] cream	600ml	1 pint	2½ cups
grated nutmeg	2.5ml	½tsp	½tsp
salt and freshly ground black pepper			

1 Cook the pasta sheets, two at a time, in a large pan of boiling salted water for 5 minutes. Remove carefully and lay on a dry towel to drain.
2 Melt the butter in a small pan and cook the onion until transparent. Tip the onion into a blender or food processor and add the cream cheese, fish, lemon juice, turmeric and egg. Season to taste with salt and pepper. Blend to a smooth purée.
3 Divide the fish mixture between the cooked pasta sheets, and spread with a knife to cover in a thin even layer. Starting with one of the short sides, roll up each sheet into a tight even roll. Wrap each roll tightly in oiled foil.
4 Steam the pasta rolls over boiling water for 15 minutes.
5 Meanwhile, make the sauce. Melt the butter in a small saucepan, add the fennel and cook over a gentle heat, stirring occasionally, for 10 minutes or until the fennel has softened. Stir in the cream, nutmeg and salt and pepper to taste and simmer gently for 2-3 minutes or until the sauce has thickened slightly.
6 When the pasta is cooked, remove the foil and cut each roll into 1cm/½ inch slices.
7 Spoon an equal quantity of the hot sauce onto 6 heated plates and place the pasta slices on top. Serve immediately.

Preparation time: 1 hour

Salad of hot fruit

Metric	Imperial	USA	
450g	1lb	1lb	firm pears, peeled, cored and cut into thin slices lengthways
1 litre	1¾ pints	1 quart	unsweetened apple juice
100g	4oz	⅔ cup	seedless raisins
1	1	1	cinnamon stick, broken into 3
225g	8oz	8oz	grapes, seedless or halved and seeded

Preparation time: about 50 minutes

1 Place the pear slices in a saucepan with the apple juice, raisins and pieces of cinnamon stick. Bring to the boil, then cover and simmer over a low heat for about 30 minutes or until the pear is tender.

2 Add the grapes and continue to simmer for 5 minutes.

3 Remove the cinnamon stick, and serve hot.

NOTE This is also very good served cold.

Corn pancakes with fried apple and Stilton sauce
Fish knots with red and green pepper sauces
and steamed leeks
Three sheets to the wind

Corn pancakes with fried apple and Stilton sauce

	Metric	Imperial	USA
flour	225g	8oz	1⅔ cups
baking powder	10ml	2tsp	2tsp
milk	275ml	9fl oz	1¼ cups
eggs	2	2	2
salt and freshly ground black pepper			
sweetcorn kernels, drained if canned or thawed if frozen	225g	8oz	1½ cups
vegetable oil for frying			
small apples, peeled, cored and cut into 18 thin slices	3	3	3
butter	50g	2oz	4tbsp
vegetable oil	15ml	1tbsp	1tbsp
Stilton cheese, mashed	100g	4oz	4oz
single [light] cream	175ml	6fl oz	¾ cup
thin slices of pickled cucumber [dill pickle], to garnish			

1 Make a smooth batter with the flour, baking powder, milk, eggs and salt and pepper to taste. Stir in the sweetcorn.
2 Heat a little oil in a frying pan over medium heat and cook 18 small pancakes, turning them over when golden on the underside. Cook 3 at a time and keep warm until you have made all the pancakes.
3 In another frying pan, fry the apple slices in the butter and oil over a low heat, just until softened. Work in manageable batches and keep warm.
4 Meanwhile, make the sauce by heating the cheese and cream in a small saucepan over a low heat until well amalgamated. Season with a little pepper.
5 To serve, place 3 pancakes topped with 3 apple slices on each hot plate. Pour over some of the sauce and decorate with a few slices of pickled cucumber.

Preparation time: 1 hour

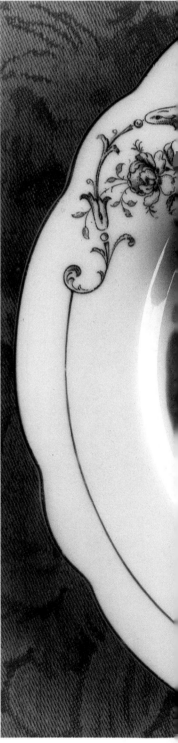

Above: Corn pancakes with fried apple and Stilton sauce; p53.
Far right: Fish knots with red and green pepper sauce and steamed leeks; p56.
Right: Three sheets to the wind; p57.

Fish knots with red and green pepper sauces and steamed leeks

Metric	Imperial	USA	
3	3	3	tail pieces of smoked cod fillet, each weighing about 225g/8oz
225g	8oz	8oz	red pepper, seeded and cut into narrow strips
225g	8oz	8oz	green pepper, seeded and cut into narrow strips
250ml	8fl oz	1 cup	chicken or vegetable stock (see page 156)
2	2	2	garlic cloves, peeled and crushed
60ml	4tbsp	4tbsp	double [heavy] cream
20ml	4tsp	4tsp	horseradish sauce, bought ready made
			salt and freshly ground black pepper
3	3	3	small leeks, trimmed and cut into 10cm/4 inch long strips

Preparation time: 1 hour

1 Cut each piece of fish lengthways into 6 long thin strips. Remove the skin from each strip with a very sharp knife, being careful not to break the flesh.

2 Carefully tie each strip into a 'knot' and secure by pushing a wooden cocktail stick through from one side to the other, if necessary. Arrange the knots on a lightly oiled plate which will fit inside a steamer. Set aside.

3 Place the strips of pepper, skin up, under a preheated grill [broiler] and leave until all the skin has blackened. Place the hot pepper strips in two plastic bags, keeping the colours separate. Leave to cool for 5 minutes, then remove from the bag and peel off the skins.

4 Put the green pepper flesh in a blender or food processor with half of the stock, 1 garlic clove, half of the cream and horseradish sauce and salt and pepper to taste. Blend until smooth, then pour into a small pan.

5 Purée the red pepper with the remaining stock, garlic, cream, horseradish sauce. Season and pour into another pan.

6 Steam the leeks for 5 minutes or until tender. Steam the fish knots for 3-4 minutes or until just cooked. Reheat the sauces.

7 To serve, very carefully remove the cocktail sticks from the fish, being careful not to break the knots. Place 3 knots down the centre of each hot plate. Place some strips of leek along either side and spoon some of the green sauce to one side and red sauce to the other. Serve immediately.

Three sheets to the wind

	Metric	Imperial	USA
white wine	600ml	1 pint	2½ cups
sugar	45ml	3tbsp	3tbsp
brandy	30ml	2tbsp	2tbsp
unflavoured gelatine	1 sachet	1 sachet	1 env.
milk	600ml	1 pint	2½ cups
egg yolks	2	2	2
cornflour [cornstarch]	15ml	1tbsp	1tbsp
vanilla essence [extract]	2.5ml	½tsp	½tsp
double [heavy] cream, lightly whipped	300ml	½ pint	1¼ cups

1 Heat half of the wine with 30ml/2tbsp of the sugar and the brandy until just boiling, stirring to dissolve the sugar. Remove from the heat and sprinkle over the gelatine. Stir over gentle heat until the gelatine is dissolved. Do not boil.

2 Mix with the rest of the wine and cool.

3 Pour into 6 wine glasses. Arrange these carefully propped on something in the refrigerator so that they are at an angle of 45° and leave to set.

4 Meanwhile, make the custard. Bring the milk almost to boiling point in a saucepan. While this is heating, whisk the egg yolks with the cornflour, remaining sugar and vanilla until pale. When the milk is almost boiling pour it in a steady stream on to the egg mixture, whisking all the time. Strain through a sieve back into the saucepan. Cook over the lowest possible heat until thickened. This custard will not go lumpy if stirred all the time it is cooking. Allow to cool.

5 Pour the custard on to the set wine jelly and return to the refrigerator at the same angle. Leave to set.

6 Just before serving, stand the glasses upright and pour in the lightly whipped cream. Serve immediately.

Preparation time: 30 minutes plus cooling and chilling

EASTERN PROMISE

ORIENTAL BANQUET Party menu for 12 people
Hot and sour soup
Pot sticker dumplings
Citrus chicken
Steamed mushroom balls
Fried noodles with vegetables
Lotus root and mandarin salad
Green fruit salad with ginger

Right: top: Fried noodles with vegetables; **centre, left to right:** Pot sticker dumplings; Hot and sour soup; Lotus root and mandarin salad; **below, left to right:** Green fruit salad with ginger; Steamed mushroom balls; Citrus chicken; pp58-64.

Hot and sour soup

Metric	Imperial	USA	
2.4 litres	4 pints	2½ quarts	chicken or vegetable stock (see page 156)
225g	8oz	8oz	chicken breast fillet, cut into thin slivers
8	8	8	dried Chinese mushrooms, soaked in a little water for 30 minutes, drained, stalks discarded and thinly sliced
175g	6oz	6oz	cooked peeled prawns [shrimp] thawed if frozen
225g	8oz	8oz	tofu (beancurd), cut into 1cm/½ inch cubes
100g	4oz	1 cup	canned bamboo shoots, cut into thin slivers
100g	4oz	1 cup	peas, thawed if frozen
4	4	4	spring onions [scallions], trimmed and chopped
60ml	4tbsp	¼ cup	soy sauce
90ml	6tbsp	6tbsp	white wine vinegar
175ml	6fl oz	¾ cup	water
60ml	4tbsp	¼ cup	cornflour [cornstarch]
			salt and freshly ground black pepper
			sesame oil

Preparation time: 1 hour

1 Bring the stock to the boil in a large saucepan. Add the chicken and mushrooms and simmer, covered, for 10 minutes.

2 Add the prawns, tofu, bamboo shoots, peas and spring onions and simmer for 2 more minutes.

3 Mix together the soy sauce, vinegar, water and cornflour in a bowl. Season with a little salt and plenty of pepper to give the soup its characteristic 'hot' flavour. Stir the mixture into the soup and cook for another 2 minutes. This will thicken the soup.

4 Pour the soup into heated bowls and add a few drops of sesame oil to each serving.

Pot sticker dumplings

Metric	Imperial	USA	
350g	12oz	2⅓ cups	flour
250ml	8fl oz	1 cup	very hot water
175g	6oz	6oz	white crab meat, drained if canned, thawed if frozen
50g	2oz	⅔ cup	white cabbage, finely chopped
2	2	2	small spring onions [scallions], trimmed and finely chopped
5-cm	2-inch	2-inch	cube fresh ginger, peeled and finely chopped
30ml	2tbsp	2tbsp	dry sherry
30ml	2tbsp	2tbsp	soy sauce
2.5ml	½tsp	½tsp	salt
10ml	2tsp	2tsp	sesame oil
5ml	1tsp	1tsp	sugar
60ml	4tbsp	¼ cup	vegetable oil
300ml	½ pint	1¼ cups	chicken or vegetable stock (see page 156)
			bottled sweet chilli sauce

Preparation time: 1½ hours

1 Make a dough with the flour and hot water. Knead for 10 minutes, adding a little more water if the dough seems too dry or more flour if too wet. Leave to rest, covered with a damp cloth, for 30 minutes.

2 Meanwhile, make the filling by mixing together the crab, cabbage, onion, ginger, sherry, soy sauce, salt, sesame oil and sugar in a bowl.

3 Knead the dough again for 5 minutes and, working in manageable batches, form into 36 equal balls. On a floured surface, roll out the balls to make rounds about 7.5cm/3 inches in diameter. Keep balls and rounds covered with a damp cloth while working.

4 Place a small teaspoonful of stuffing in the centre of each round of dough. Dampen the edges with water, fold over to make a semi-circle and pinch the edges to seal. Now 'frill' the edges and make each dumpling into a small semi-circular shape with the 'frilly' seam on top and a flat bottom.

5 Heat the oil in a large sauté pan (if you don't have one large enough to take the dumplings all in one layer, work in two batches). Fry the dumplings over a very low heat for 2 minutes or until their flat bottoms are crisp and golden.

6 Pour on the stock, cover and simmer over very low heat for 12-15 minutes or until almost all the liquid has been absorbed. Remove the lid and cook for a further 2 minutes.

7 To serve, place 3 dumplings on each plate with a little chilli sauce.

Citrus chicken

	Metric	Imperial	USA
egg whites, lightly beaten	3	3	3
cornflour [cornstarch]	45ml	3tbsp	3tbsp
chicken breast fillets, cut into 1cm/½ inch strips	700g	1½lb	1½lb
vegetable oil for deep frying			
chicken or vegetable stock (see page 156)	250ml	8fl oz	1 cup
lemon juice	75ml	5tbsp	5tbsp
sugar	30ml	2tbsp	2tbsp
light soy sauce	30ml	2tbsp	2tbsp
sherry	30ml	2tbsp	2tbsp
garlic cloves, peeled and crushed	2	2	2
chilli powder	5ml	1tsp	1tsp
vegetable oil	30ml	2tbsp	2tbsp
small green pepper, cored, seeded and cut into small dice	1	1	1
water	15ml	1tbsp	1tbsp

1 Mix the egg whites and 30ml/2tbsp cornflour thoroughly in a bowl, then mix in the chicken strips, making sure that they are all coated with the mixture. Cover closely and refrigerate for 30 minutes.

Preparation time: 1 hour

2 Deep fry the chicken strips for 1 minute, drain and keep warm.

3 Mix together the stock, lemon juice, sugar, soy sauce, sherry, garlic and chilli powder.

4 Heat the 30ml/2tbsp oil in a wok or large frying pan and stir-fry the green pepper for 2 minutes over a medium heat. Stir in the stock mixture and simmer 1 minute.

5 Mix the remaining cornflour with the water, add to the pan and simmer 1 minute, stirring.

6 Add the chicken to pan and cook for a further 30 seconds, stirring. Make sure all the chicken pieces are coated with sauce. Serve immediately.

Lotus root and mandarin salad

Metric	Imperial	USA	
2×540g	2×19oz	2×19oz	cans sliced lotus root, drained (if sliced lotus root is unavailable, buy lotus root pieces, drain and slice thinly)
12	12	12	small mandarin oranges or tangerines, peeled and thinly sliced crossways
2.5-cm	1-inch	1-inch	cube fresh ginger, peeled and crushed through a garlic press
			double quantity vinaigrette dressing (see page 158)
6	6	6	spring onions [scallions], trimmed and cut into julienne strips

Preparation time: 25 minutes

1 In a large bowl, combine the slices of lotus root with the mandarin slices.
2 Stir the crushed ginger into the dressing and pour over the salad. Mix carefully so as not to break the lotus root slices.
3 Place in a serving bowl or dish and garnish with the onions.

Steamed mushroom balls

Metric	Imperial	USA	
2	2	2	dried Chinese mushrooms, soaked in a little water for 30 minutes, drained, stalks discarded and very finely chopped
100g	4oz	¾ cup	mushrooms, finely chopped
1	1	1	small onion, peeled and very finely chopped
75g	3oz	½ cup	canned water chestnuts, very finely chopped
1	1	1	garlic clove, peeled and crushed
15ml	1tbsp	1tbsp	cornflour [cornstarch]
50g	2oz	1 cup	fresh white breadcrumbs
2.5cm	1-inch	1-inch	cube fresh ginger, peeled and very finely chopped
10ml	2tsp	2tsp	soy sauce
4	4	4	eggs, beaten
			flour
225g	8oz	1 cup	short-grain rice, soaked in cold water for 1 hour, drained and thoroughly dried on towels
			bottled sweet chilli sauce
			bottled Chinese plum sauce or hoi sin sauce (Chinese barbecue sauce)

Preparation time: 1¼ hours

1 Mix both kinds of mushrooms with the onion, water chestnuts, garlic, cornflour, breadcrumbs, ginger, soy sauce and 2 of the beaten eggs.
2 Form the mixture into 24 small balls. Working very gently, dip each ball first in flour, then in the remaining beaten eggs and then roll in the dried rice to coat.
3 Arrange the balls in steamers, leaving a little space between each for the rice to swell.

4 Steam for 20 minutes.

5 Serve with the chilli sauce and plum or barbecue sauce as dips.

NOTE The mixture should be very moist; however, if it is too wet to form into balls, shake in a fine sieve so that the excess liquid drains away.

Fried noodles with vegetables

	Metric	Imperial	USA
vegetable oil	60ml	4tbsp	¼ cup
onions, peeled and chopped	2	2	2
garlic cloves, peeled and crushed	3	3	3
2.5cm/1 inch cubes fresh ginger, peeled and finely chopped	2	2	2
can baby corn-on-the-cob, drained and cut into bite-size pieces, or sweetcorn kernels	400g	14oz	16oz
canned water chestnuts, drained and sliced	175g	6oz	6oz
mange-touts [snow peas], trimmed and cut into bite-size pieces	175g	6oz	6oz
bean sprouts	175g	6oz	6oz
dried Chinese noodles, boiled for 5 minutes and drained	450g	1lb	1lb
sesame oil	10ml	2tsp	2tsp

1 Heat a wok or large frying pan over a high heat, add the oil and when hot, add the onions. Stir-fry for 2 minutes, then add the garlic, ginger, sweetcorn, water chestnuts and mange-touts. Stir-fry for 2 minutes. Add the bean sprouts and stir-fry for 1 minute. Add the noodles and stir-fry for 2 minutes longer or until the noodles are hot and the vegetables are distributed evenly through them.

2 Tip the contents of the pan into a heated serving dish and drizzle over the sesame oil.

NOTE The noodles can be cooked up to an hour before they are needed and kept in a large bowl of cold water. Drain well before adding to the vegetable mixture.

Preparation time: 30 minutes

Green fruit salad with ginger

Metric	Imperial	USA	
1 litre	1¾ pints	1 quart	white grape juice
30ml	2tbsp	2tbsp	green ginger wine (optional)
4	4	4	green-skinned apples, cored and cut into very thin rings
450g	1lb	1lb	green grapes, seedless or halved and seeded
4	4	4	kiwi fruit, peeled and sliced thinly crossways
12	12	12	fresh lychees, peeled, or canned and drained
2	2	2	star fruit or carambola sliced crossways (optional)
200g	7oz	¾ cup	preserved ginger in syrup, cut into thin slices
30ml	2tbsp	2tbsp	syrup from preserved ginger

Preparation time: 20 minutes plus chilling

Combine all the ingredients in a large bowl, cover closely and chill for at least 2 hours for the flavour to develop.

South China Seas salad
Balinese duck
Marbled tea eggs
Banana pancakes

South China Seas salad

Metric	Imperial	USA	
6	6	6	spring onions [scallions]
225g	8oz	8oz	bean sprouts
1	1	1	bunch radishes, trimmed and sliced if large
225-g	8-oz	8-oz	can water chestnuts, drained
225-g	8-oz	8-oz	can bamboo shoots, drained and sliced
450g	1lb	1lb	cooked peeled prawns [shrimp], thawed if frozen
300g	6oz	6oz	tofu (beancurd)
			chilli sauce
			soy sauce

Preparation time: 20 minutes

1 Trim the spring onions, removing most of the green part, and make a cut with a sharp knife lengthways from the bulb along the length. Make another cut at right-angles to the first, leaving the bulb intact. Place in a bowl of iced water.

2 Arrange the bean sprouts, radishes, water chestnuts, bamboo shoots and prawns in small bowls (or on plates). Tuck the onions into the salad to curl over the edge of the bowl.

3 Purée the tofu in a blender or food processor and flavour with chilli and soy sauce to taste. Drizzle over the salads.

Balinese duck

	Metric	Imperial	USA
duck, with giblets	1.8-2kg	4-4½lb	4-4½lb
salt	7.5ml	1½tsp	1½tsp
chilli powder	2.5ml	½tsp	½tsp
ground cumin	2.5ml	½tsp	½tsp
ground coriander	2.5ml	½tsp	½tsp
desiccated [shredded dried] coconut, soaked in 450ml/ ¾ pint [2 cups] boiling water for 30 minutes	75g	3oz	1 cup
vegetable oil	15ml	1tbsp	1tbsp
small onion, peeled and chopped	1	1	1
garlic clove, peeled and crushed	1	1	1
cube fresh ginger, peeled and crushed through a garlic press	2.5-cm	1-inch	1-inch
small fresh red chilli, seeded and very finely chopped, or 2.5ml/½tsp additional chilli powder	1	1	1
grated rind and juice of 1 small lemon			
brown sugar	10ml	2tsp	2tsp
soy sauce	10ml	2tsp	2tsp
steamed rice			
fried onion rings, to garnish			
marbled tea eggs, quartered (see following recipe)	6	6	6

1 6-12 hours before cooking, having removed the giblets, pour a large kettle of boiling water over the duck. This will tighten the skin. Dry thoroughly inside and out. Place on a rack and leave to dry in a draughty place for 6-12 hours.

2 Put the giblets in a small pan, cover with water and bring to the boil, skimming off any scum which rises to the surface. Cover and simmer for 1 hour. Discard the giblets and boil the stock hard until reduced to 30ml/2tbsp. Set aside.

3 Mix 5ml/1tsp salt, the chilli powder, cumin and coriander together and rub all over the duck skin. Prick the duck all over with a needle or small skewer to allow the fat to run out during cooking. Place the bird on a rack over a roasting pan and roast in the oven for about 2 hours. The meat will be cooked and the skin very crisp and golden.

4 Meanwhile, make the sauce. Strain the coconut 'milk' through a sieve into a bowl, pressing the coconut to extract all the liquid. Discard the coconut.

5 Heat the oil in a saucepan and cook the onion until transparent. Add the garlic, ginger, chopped chilli or chilli powder, lemon rind and juice, sugar, coconut 'milk', reduced stock, soy sauce and remaining salt. Bring to the boil, stirring, then cover the pan and simmer gently for 30 minutes.

Oven temperature: 180°C/ 350°F/Gas Mark 4
Preparation time: 4 hours plus drying

6 When the duck is cooked, remove it from the oven and allow it to rest for 15 minutes. Remove all the skin from the duck, cut it into bite-size pieces and keep warm. Remove all meat from the duck and cut into bite-size pieces. Toss the duck pieces in the sauce to coat.

7 To serve, place some steamed rice on each hot plate and garnish with the fried onion rings. Next to this arrange some of the duck in sauce, with the crispy skin on top. Lastly, add the egg quarters. Serve immediately.

Marbled tea eggs

Metric	Imperial	USA	
6	6	6	eggs, hard boiled
			pot of very strong Indian tea
30ml	2tbsp	2tbsp	dark soy sauce

Preparation time: 1 hour 10 minutes plus cooling

1 Gently bash the hard-boiled eggs all over so the shells are covered in small cracks.

2 Place in a saucepan, cover with tea and add the soy sauce. Simmer for 1 hour.

3 Drain and cool. Before serving, shell and quarter.

Banana pancakes [crêpes]

Metric	Imperial	USA	
100g	4oz	¾ cup	flour
			pinch of salt
1	1	1	large banana, peeled and mashed
2	2	2	eggs, beaten
200ml	⅓ pint	1 cup	milk
			vegetable oil for frying
			sugar
			lemon juice

Preparation time: 15 minutes plus resting

1 Make a smooth batter with the flour, salt, banana, eggs and milk. Leave to rest for 1 hour.

2 Brush a 20cm/8 inch frying pan with a little oil and heat, then make 6 pancakes [crêpes] in the usual way, turning once. Cook over a lowish heat to give the centre time to cook through. Stack and keep warm as cooked.

3 To serve, place a pancakes [crêpes] on each hot plate and sprinkle with sugar and lemon juice to taste.

Above: South China Seas salad; p64.
Right: Balinese duck and Marbled tea eggs; pp65/6.

Tempura vegetables
Sweet and sour pickles
Stuffed tofu
Stir-fry salad
Guava fool

Tempura vegetables

Metric	Imperial	USA	
1	1	1	egg, beaten
1	1	1	egg yolk, beaten
175ml	6fl oz	¾ cup	water
100g	4oz	¾ cup	flour
12	12	12	sticks of peeled parsnip, 5mm×7.5cm/¼×3 inches
12	12	12	tiny mushrooms, or slices of larger mushroom
12	12	12	onion rings
			vegetable oil for deep frying

Preparation time: 20 minutes

1 Make a smooth batter with the egg, egg yolk, water and flour.
2 Dip the pieces of vegetable in the batter, a few at a time, and fry very quickly in hot oil, turning once. Remove stray bits of batter from the oil from time to time.
3 Drain on paper towels and serve immediately with sweet and sour pickles (see following recipe).
NOTE The variety and quantities of the vegetables are merely a suggestion. It is most important, however, that all vegetables used should be young and in peak condition, as they are barely cooked when eaten. These should be served to your guests as they come from the pan in small batches. Do not attempt to keep them warm or they will lose their crispness.

Sweet and sour pickles

Metric	Imperial	USA	
50g	2oz	½ cup	white cabbage, shredded
1	1	1	small onion, peeled and shredded
50g	2oz	2oz	white radish (mooli or daikon) or turnip, peeled and cut into tiny sticks
½	½	½	small carrot, peeled and cut into tiny sticks
½	½	½	small green pepper, cored, seeded and cut into tiny sticks
½	½	½	small red pepper, cored and seeded and cut into tiny sticks

water	300ml	½ pint	1¼ cups
vinegar	300ml	½ pint	1¼ cups
salt	2.5ml	½tsp	½tsp
chilli powder	1.25ml	¼tsp	¼tsp
sugar	30ml	2tbsp	2tbsp

1 Place all the ingredients in a saucepan, bring to the boil and simmer, covered, for 2 minutes.

2 Leave to cool, still covered. As soon as it has cooled, this pickle is ready to serve. The remainder can be stored for later use in airtight jars, covered with the cooking liquid.

Preparation time: 1 hour plus cooling

Stuffed tofu

	Metric	Imperial	USA
firm tofu (beancurd), cut into 6 square pieces each about 3cm/1¼ inches thick	1.25kg	2½lb	2½lb
cornflour [cornstarch] for dredging			
vegetable oil	75ml	5tbsp	5tbsp
chicken or vegetable stock (see page 156)	350ml	12floz	1½ cups
salt	5ml	1tsp	1tsp
Chinese oyster sauce	30ml	2tbsp	2tbsp
cornflour [cornstarch] mixed with a little water	10ml	2tsp	2tsp
spring onions [scallions], trimmed and sliced	3	3	3

The stuffing

minced [ground] chicken	175g	6oz	¾ cup
finely chopped onion	15ml	1tbsp	1tbsp
light soy sauce	30ml	2tbsp	2tbsp
dry sherry	5ml	1tsp	1tsp
cornflour [cornstarch]	10ml	2tsp	2tsp

1 Mix together the chicken, onion, soy sauce, sherry and cornflour to make the stuffing.

2 Cut each piece of firm tofu in half diagonally to make 12 triangles. With a sharp knife, cut a slit in the long side of each triangle and scoop out a little of the tofu to make a pocket for stuffing. Be very careful not to cut too deeply, and work very carefully as the tofu is very fragile.

3 Dust each 'pocket' with a little cornflour and carefully fill with the stuffing.

4 Heat the oil in a wide pan (a sauté pan is ideal, but if you do not have a

Preparation time: 1 hour

pan wide enough to take all the triangles in one layer, cook them in two batches, keeping the first batch warm while you cook the rest). Place the triangles in the pan stuffing side down (with the opposite point upwards) and cook over a low heat until the stuffing is golden brown, about 5 minutes.

5 Pour in the stock, cover and cook for a further 3 minutes. Remove the tofu from the pan and keep warm.

6 Add the salt, oyster sauce and cornflour mixture to the pan and simmer, stirring, until thickened.

7 To serve, arrange 2 triangles of tofu on each of 6 hot plates, pour over the sauce and garnish with spring onion. Serve with plain steamed rice and stir-fry salad (see following recipe).

Stir-fry salad

Metric	Imperial	USA	
30ml	2tbsp	2tbsp	vegetable oil
5ml	1tsp	1tsp	sesame oil
175g	6oz	3 cups	Chinese leaves [Nappa or celery cabbage], or crisp lettuce, shredded
175g	6oz	4 cups	bean sprouts
1	1	1	garlic clove, peeled and crushed
2.5-cm	1-inch	1-inch	cube fresh ginger, peeled and finely chopped
10ml	2tsp	2tsp	soy sauce

Preparation time: 10 minutes

1 Heat the oils in a wok or large frying pan over a high heat. Add the greens and bean sprouts with the garlic and ginger and stir-fry for about 3 minutes or until the greens are hot.

2 Add the soy sauce and continue to stir-fry for 30 seconds. Serve immediately.

Guava fool

Metric	Imperial	USA	
415-g	14½-oz	16-oz	can guavas, drained
			juice of ½ lemon
300ml	½ pint	1¼ cups	double [heavy] cream, whipped until stiff

Preparation time: 10 minutes plus chilling

1 Slice 1 guava thinly crossways and reserve for garnish.

2 Purée the remaining fruit with the lemon juice in a blender or food processor and fold into the whipped cream. Spoon into 6 bowls, glasses or plates and chill at least 1 hour.

3 Garnish each serving with a little sliced guava and serve.

NOTE If you can find fresh guavas, so much the better!

Above: Tempura
vegetables with Sweet
and sour pickles; p68.
Right: Stuffed tofu; p69.

Terrine of curried vegetables with lime pickle sorbet
Five-spice battered prawns with coconut anise sauce
Cellophane noodles
Salad of green leaves and lychees
with ginger dressing

Terrine of curried vegetables with lime pickle sorbet

Metric	Imperial	USA	
350g	12oz	12oz	carrots, scraped and cut into chunks
350g	12oz	12oz	cauliflower, cut into florets
4	4	4	eggs
30ml	2tbsp	2tbsp	double [heavy] cream
7.5ml	1½tsp	1½tsp	good curry powder
			salt and freshly ground black pepper
			slices of pickled gherkin, to garnish
		The sorbet	
600ml	1 pint	2½ cups	vegetable or chicken stock (see page 156)
10ml	2tsp	2tsp	Indian mild lime pickle
1	1	1	egg white, beaten

Oven temperature: 200°C/
400°F/Gas Mark 6
Preparation time: 1¼ hours
plus chilling and freezing

1 Boil or steam the carrots and cauliflower until tender, keeping them separate. Allow to cool.

2 Purée the cooked cauliflower in a blender or food processor with 2 eggs and half of the cream and curry powder. Season to taste with salt and pepper. Pour into a well-oiled 900ml/1½ pint [1-quart] capacity loaf pan or mould.

3 Repeat the process with the carrots and remaining eggs, cream and curry powder. Pour this orange purée over the white purée already in the pan.

4 Cover tightly with oiled foil and cook in a bain-marie in the oven for 40 minutes.

5 Allow to cool and then chill for several hours.

6 To make the sorbet, blend the stock and pickle in a blender or food processor, then pour into a shallow freezerproof container. Freeze until half frozen and slushy. Remove from the freezer from time to time during this period and break up the ice crystals which begin to form around the edges.

7 When slushy mix well once more with a fork and fold in the beaten egg white. Freeze again until firm. Transfer the sorbet to the refrigerator 1 hour before required or it will be too hard to serve.

8 To serve, place a thick slice of terrine on each plate, garnish with gherkin slices and spoon some sorbet around it.

NOTE This dish is even more unusual if the terrine is served hot.

Five-spice battered prawns with coconut anise sauce

	Metric	Imperial	USA
water	300ml	½ pint	1¼ cups
milk	300ml	½ pint	1¼ cups
desiccated [shredded dried] coconut	175g	6oz	2 cups
star anise	1	1	1
vegetable oil	15ml	1tbsp	1tbsp
small onion, peeled and chopped	1	1	1
garlic clove, peeled and crushed	1	1	1
cube fresh ginger, peeled and finely chopped	1-cm	½-inch	½-inch
cornflour [cornstarch], dissolved in a little water	15ml	1tbsp	1tbsp
juice of ½ lemon			
salt and freshly ground black pepper			
pinch of chilli powder			
large shelled prawns [jumbo shrimp]	350g	12oz	12oz
oil for deep frying			

The batter

flour	150g	5oz	1 cup
cornflour [cornstarch]	75ml	5tbsp	5tbsp
baking powder	7.5ml	1½tsp	1½tsp
Chinese 5-spice powder	2.5ml	½tsp	½tsp
water	275ml	9fl oz	1¼ cups
salt	2.5ml	½tsp	½tsp
vegetable oil	30ml	2tbsp	2tbsp

1 To make the batter, mix the flour, cornflour, baking powder and 5-spice powder in a bowl. Add the water and beat to a smooth batter. Leave to rest for 1 hour. Just before using, beat in the salt and oil.

2 Put the water, milk and coconut in a saucepan with the star anise, and slowly bring to the boil. Remove from the heat and leave to infuse for 1 hour. Press the contents of the pan through a fine sieve, pressing the solids with the back of a wooden spoon to extract as much 'milk' as possible. Discard the solids in the sieve.

3 Heat the oil in a saucepan and cook the onion until transparent. Add the garlic and ginger and continue to cook for 1-2 minutes.

Preparation time: 45 minutes plus resting and infusing

4 Place the onion mixture in a blender or food processor with the coconut 'milk', cornflour and lemon juice. Season to taste with salt, pepper and chilli powder. Blend until smooth. Pour into the pan and cook for 5 minutes over a low heat, stirring occasionally; the sauce will thicken. If too thick, thin with a little cream.

5 Dip the prawns in the batter and deep fry in small batches until golden brown and crisp. Drain on paper towels and keep the cooked prawns warm in the oven while the rest are being cooked. Work quickly.

6 To serve, quickly arrange the prawns on 6 hot plates or bowls and pour some of the sauce over them. Serve immediately.

NOTE This dish is even better made with uncooked prawns. Remove their heads and shells before dipping in batter.

Right: Terrine of curried vegetables with lime pickle sorbet; p72.
Far right: top: Salad of green leaves and lychees with ginger dressing; **centre:** Cellophane noodles; **below:** Five-spice battered prawns with coconut anise sauce; pp73–76.

Cellophane noodles

Metric	Imperial	USA	
15ml	1tbsp	1tbsp	vegetable oil
3	3	3	small onions, peeled and cut into thin strips
3	3	3	garlic cloves, peeled and crushed
400ml	⅔ pint	1¾ cups	vegetable or chicken stock (see page 156)
30ml	2tbsp	2tbsp	Chinese black bean sauce
30ml	2tbsp	2tbsp	light soy sauce
5ml	1tsp	1tsp	chilli powder
100g	4oz	4oz	cellophane noodles, soaked in hot water for 10 minutes and drained
5ml	1tsp	1tsp	sesame oil

Preparation time: 30 minutes

1 Heat the oil in a wok or large frying pan over a medium heat and stir-fry the onions for 2 minutes. Add the garlic, stock, black bean sauce, soy sauce and chilli powder and simmer for 5 minutes.

2 Add the noodles and cook for 2 minutes, stirring constantly – the noodles will absorb most of liquid. Sprinkle over the sesame oil and serve at once.

Salad of green leaves and lychees with ginger dressing

Metric	Imperial	USA	
			an assortment of green salad leaves, eg 2 kinds of lettuce, watercress, chicory [Belgian endive] and Chinese leaves [Nappa or celery cabbage]
567-g	20-oz	20-oz	can lychees, drained
			The dressing
45ml	3tbsp	3tbsp	vegetable oil
7.5ml	1½tsp	1½tsp	sesame oil
15ml	1tbsp	1tbsp	lemon juice
1	1	1	garlic clove, peeled and crushed
2.5-cm	1-inch	1-inch	cube fresh ginger, peeled and crushed through a garlic press
10ml	2tsp	2tsp	sugar
			salt and freshly ground black pepper

Preparation time: 15-20 minutes

1 Wash and dry the salad greens and tear into small pieces. Place in a large bowl.

2 Mix all the dressing ingredients thoroughly, pour over the salad and toss well.

3 Divide the greens between 6 bowls or plates and arrange the lychees on top. Serve immediately.

NOTE If you can find fresh lychees, these are of course better flavoured than canned ones.

Turkish stuffed mussels with egg and lemon sauce
Apricot and walnut chicken
Aubergine mousse
Three pepper salad
Turkish yogurt fool

Turkish stuffed mussels with egg and lemon sauce

	Metric	Imperial	USA
olive oil	15ml	1tbsp	1tbsp
onion, peeled and chopped	1	1	1
garlic clove, peeled and crushed	1	1	1
pine nuts	25g	1oz	¼ cup
currants	25g	1oz	3tbsp
long grain rice	50g	2oz	⅓ cup
chopped parsley	45ml	3tbsp	3tbsp
chicken or vegetable stock (see page 156)	300ml	½ pint	1¼ cups
salt and freshly ground black pepper			
live mussels, cleaned and opened (see page 9) but left in shells	48	48	48
water	600ml	1 pint	2½ cups
egg yolks	2	2	2
juice of 1 lemon			

1 Heat the oil in a saucepan and fry the onion until transparent. Add the garlic, pine nuts, currants, rice and 15ml/1 tbsp parsley. Cook, stirring, for 1 minute. Pour over the stock just to cover. Cover the pan tightly and cook over a very low heat until all the water is absorbed and the rice is tender. Cool, and season to taste with salt and pepper.

2 Divide the rice mixture between the mussels, pressing it into the empty half of each shell. Close and tie each shell firmly shut with thin string or cotton thread.

3 Pack the mussels closely together into a medium saucepan. Pour over the water. Bring to the boil, then cover and simmer gently for 30 minutes.

4 Remove the mussels from the pan with a slotted spoon. Remove the string and keep warm.

5 Mix the egg yolks with the lemon juice and add to the liquid in the pan. Heat, whisking constantly, until the sauce thickens – do not allow it to boil or the eggs will scramble. Add the remaining parsley, and season to taste with salt and pepper.

Preparation time: 2 hours plus cooling

Far right: top: Three pepper salad; **below:** Apricot and walnut chicken with Aubergine [eggplant] mousse; pp80/81.

Below: Turkish stuffed mussels with egg and lemon sauce; p77.

6 To serve, place 8 mussels in each heated soup plate or shallow bowl, pour over the sauce and serve, with bread to mop up the juices.

NOTE The job of tying the mussels is much easier and quicker than it sounds, but you really do need two pairs of hands. Have all the lengths of thread or string cut ready to the correct length. For a special occasion, tie 2 or 3 mussels per person with coloured thread and leave these tied for the guests to open themselves. Any stuffing left over is delicious eaten cold as a salad.

Apricot and walnut chicken

Metric	Imperial	USA	
75g	3oz	6tbsp	butter
½	½	½	small onion, peeled and chopped
50g	2oz	⅓ cup	dried apricots, soaked for 6 hours, drained and finely chopped
1	1	1	garlic clove, peeled and crushed
15ml	1tbsp	1tbsp	chopped parsley
10ml	2tsp	2tsp	lemon juice
			salt and freshly ground black pepper
3×175g	3×6oz	3×6oz	large chicken breast fillets flattened until thin
			flour
1	1	1	egg, beaten
100g	4oz	1 cup	walnuts, finely chopped
			The sauce
300ml	½ pint	1¼ cups	single [light] cream
2	2	2	garlic cloves, peeled and crushed
25g	1oz	3tbsp	dried apricots, soaked for 6 hours, drained and finely chopped

Preparation time: 45 minutes
plus soaking

1 Melt 25g/1oz [2tbsp] butter in a small saucepan and cook the onion and apricots, stirring occasionally, until the onion is transparent. Add the garlic, parsley and lemon juice and season to taste with salt and pepper. Cook for 1 minute over medium heat, stirring. Allow to cool.

2 Divide between the flattened chicken breasts and fold them over like omelettes. Secure with wooden cocktail sticks to hold in the stuffing. Dip first in flour, then beaten eggs and then in chopped nuts to coat, being careful not to lose any of the stuffing.

3 Melt the remaining butter in a frying pan and cook the stuffed breasts over low heat for 3-4 minutes on each side or until just cooked through. Remove from the pan, carefully remove the wooden cocktail sticks and cut crossways into 1cm/½ inch slices. Keep warm.

4 To make the sauce, heat the cream with the garlic and chopped apricots for 2-3 minutes over very gentle heat. Season to taste with salt and pepper.

5 To serve, divide the slices of stuffed chicken between 6 heated plates. Pour over the sauce. Add aubergine mousse (see following recipe) and cooked seasonal vegetables. Serve immediately.

Aubergine mousse

Metric	Imperial	USA	
450g	1lb	1lb	aubergines [eggplants]
3	3	3	eggs
120ml	4floz	½ cup	double [heavy] cream
			salt and freshly ground black pepper

1 Prick the skins of the aubergines and bake in the oven until quite soft. The time will depend on the size of the vegetable. Cool.
2 Remove the flesh from the aubergines and place in a sieve; discard the skins. Drain for 30 minutes, then press the flesh with a wooden spoon against the sieve to extract any excess moisture.
3 Purée the drained aubergine flesh with the eggs and cream in a blender or food processor. Season to taste with salt and pepper.
4 Line the bottoms of 6 buttered ramekins or ovenproof moulds with circles of greaseproof [parchment] paper, which has been buttered on both sides. Pour in the aubergine mixture and bake in a bain-marie in the oven for about 45 minutes or until set.
5 Run a knife around each mousse to loosen it, then turn it out and remove the paper. Garnish with red pepper shapes, if liked.

Oven temperature: 220°C/ 425°F/Gas Mark 7, then 160°C/ 325°F/Gas Mark 3
Preparation time: about 2¼ hours

Three pepper salad

	Metric	Imperial	USA
large red pepper, cored, seeded and cut into tiny dice	1	1	1
large green pepper, cored, seeded and cut into tiny dice	1	1	1
quantity of vinaigrette dressing (see page 158)	1	1	1
green peppercorns	10ml	2tsp	2tsp

Combine all the ingredients in a bowl. Toss and leave to marinate at room temperature for 1-2 hours, to allow flavours to develop.

Preparation time: 10-15 minutes plus marinating

Turkish yogurt fool

	Metric	Imperial	USA
thick Greek-style yogurt	240g	8½oz	1 cup
double [heavy] cream	300ml	½ pint	1¼ cups
good-quality Turkish Delight	225g	8oz	8oz
flaked [slivered] almonds			

1 Whisk the yogurt lightly in a bowl and fold in the cream.
2 Chop the Turkish Delight into small pieces (dipping the knife in icing [confectioners'] sugar helps stop the pieces sticking together). Reserve a few pieces for garnish and fold the rest into the yogurt mixture.
3 Spoon into serving dishes or glasses and sprinkle with flaked almonds and the reserved pieces of Turkish Delight. Chill at least 1 hour.

Preparation time: 15 minutes plus chilling

FAST FEASTS

ALL-SEASON BARBEQUE Party menu for 12 people
Chestnut soup
Fish kebabs
Veggie burgers
Fresh tomato ketchup
Baked potatoes with garlic butter
Orange, olive and onion salad
Athol brose

Right : top right, and then clockwise: Baked potatoes with garlic butter; Fish kebabs; Orange, olive and onion salad; Chestnut soup; Athole brose; **centre:** Veggie burger; pp82-86.

Chestnut soup

Metric	Imperial	USA	
50g	2oz	4tbsp	butter
30ml	2tbsp	2tbsp	vegetable oil
2	2	2	large onions, peeled and chopped
4	4	4	garlic cloves, peeled and crushed
2.5ml	½tsp	½tsp	dried sage, or 5ml/1tsp chopped fresh sage if available
			salt and freshly ground black pepper
575-g	1¼-lb	1¼-lb	canned unsweetened chestnut purée
3 litres	5 pints	3 quarts	chicken or vegetable stock (see page 156)

Preparation time: 20 minutes

1 Melt the butter with the oil in a large saucepan and cook the onions over a medium heat until transparent.
2 Add the garlic and sage and season to taste with salt and black pepper. Cook, stirring, for 1 minute more, then stir in the chestnut purée and stock. Bring to the boil and simmer gently for 5 minutes, stirring constantly so that the purée melts into the soup. Serve hot.

Fish kebabs

Metric	Imperial	USA	
1.5kg	3lb	3lb	skinless filleted firm fish, such as salmon, fresh tuna, monkfish, turbot, halibut, cut into 4cm/1½ inch cubes
60ml	4tbsp	¼ cup	olive oil
30ml	2tbsp	2tbsp	lemon juice
			salt and freshly ground black pepper

Preparation time: ½ hour plus marinating

1 Put the fish cubes in a bowl, add the remaining ingredients and stir to mix. Leave to marinate for about 1 hour, stirring occasionally.
2 Thread the fish cubes on to metal skewers.
3 Cook on a barbecue (not too near the coals), or under a preheated grill [broiler], for about 3 minutes on each side or until the fish is just cooked through.
NOTE Mackerel would make a tasty *cheap* alternative to the fish suggested above.

Veggie burgers

Metric	Imperial	USA	
45ml	3tbsp	3tbsp	olive oil
2	2	2	large onions, peeled and chopped
225g	8oz	1 cup	carrots, scraped and finely chopped
225g	8oz	2 cups	mushrooms, wiped and finely chopped
4	4	4	dried Chinese or Italian mushrooms, soaked in warm water for 30 minutes, drained, hard stem discarded and finely chopped
4	4	4	garlic cloves, peeled and crushed
60ml	4tbsp	¼ cup	chopped parsley or other fresh or dried herbs, to taste
4	4	4	spring onions [scallions], trimmed and finely chopped
350g	12oz	2 cups	porridge oats [oatmeal]
30ml	2tbsp	2tbsp	pine nuts or chopped mixed nuts
60ml	4tbsp	¼ cup	currants
3	3	3	eggs, beaten
			salt and freshly ground black pepper
			buns, to serve

Preparation time: 1 hour plus cooling

1 Heat the oil in a small saucepan and cook the onion for 2 minutes over a very low heat. Add the carrots, mushrooms, dried mushrooms and garlic. Cover tightly and cook gently for 10 minutes, shaking the pan occasionally and being careful that the vegetables do not stick or burn.
2 Tip the vegetables into a large bowl and let cool. Then add the

remaining ingredients and mix together thoroughly.

3 Shape into 12 equal balls and then flatten into burger shapes measuring about 9cm/3½ inches across.

4 Handling them very gently as they will be quite moist and fragile, cook the burgers for 5-7 minutes on each side on a barbecue (not too near the coals) or on a piece of oiled foil under a preheated moderate grill [broiler]. Alternatively, fry in a little vegetable oil in a large frying pan over a low heat for about 5 minutes on each side or until cooked right through.

5 Serve in buns with fresh tomato ketchup (see following recipe).

Fresh tomato ketchup

	Metric	Imperial	USA
olive oil	30ml	2tbsp	2tbsp
onion, peeled and chopped	1	1	1
garlic cloves, peeled and crushed	4	4	4
ripe tomatoes, roughly chopped	900g	2lb	2lb
chopped fresh basil or parsley, or 10ml/2tsp dried oregano	30ml	2tbsp	2tbsp
sugar	15ml	1tbsp	1tbsp
vinegar	60ml	4tbsp	¼ cup
concentrated tomato purée [paste]	30ml	2tbsp	2tbsp
water	30ml	2tbsp	2tbsp
dash of Worcestershire sauce			
salt and freshly ground black pepper			

1 Heat the oil in a saucepan and cook the onion over a medium heat until transparent. Add all the remaining ingredients, bring to the boil and simmer, covered, for 10 minutes.

2 Purée the sauce in a blender or food processor, then press through a fine sieve using the back of a wooden spoon. Discard the solids in the sieve. Allow the sauce to cool before serving.

Preparation time: 30 minutes plus cooling

Baked potatoes with garlic butter

	Metric	Imperial	USA
large baking potatoes	12	12	12
salt and freshly ground black pepper			
garlic cloves, peeled and each cut into 3 pieces	4	4	4
butter	100g	4oz	8tbsp

1 Cut each potato in half lengthways. With a teaspoon scoop out a little of the potato in the centre of each half.

2 Into each hole, spoon a little salt and pepper, a piece of garlic and a small

Oven temperature: 190°C/ 375°F/Gas Mark 5
Preparation time: 1½-2 hours

nut of butter. Replace the two halves together and wrap the potatoes very tightly in foil.

3 Bake in the oven, or on a barbecue or bonfire, until tender. (The time will depend on the method of cooking and heat of fire.)

4 Serve in the foil.

Orange, olive and onion salad

Metric	Imperial	USA	
6	6	6	large oranges, peeled and sliced thinly crossways
2	2	2	large mild onions, peeled and cut into thin rings
275g	10oz	2 cups	small black olives
			double quantity of vinaigrette dressing (see page 158)

Preparation time: 20 minutes plus marinating

Toss the oranges, onions and olives in the dressing. Leave to marinate at room temperature for 1 hour (time permitting), to allow the flavours to develop.

Athol brose

Metric	Imperial	USA	
150ml	¼ pint	⅔ cup	Scotch whisky
60ml	4tbsp	¼ cup	lemon juice
60ml	4tbsp	¼ cup	honey
600ml	1 pint	2½ cups	double [heavy] cream
75g	3oz	½ cup	ground almonds
100g	4oz	⅔ cup	porridge oats [oatmeal], browned for 2-3 minutes under grill [broiler], shaking occasionally
			flaked [slivered] almonds, to decorate

Preparation time: 15 minutes plus chilling

1 Mix the whisky with the lemon juice and honey in a bowl. Add the cream and whisk until the mixture will form peaks.

2 Gently fold in the ground almonds, then the toasted oats. Spoon into 12 glasses or dishes or 1 large bowl. Chill for at least 1 hour.

3 Sprinkle with flaked almonds just before serving.

Right: Asparagus omelette with Purée of broad beans and Green salad; pp88/89.

Smoked fish mousse
Asparagus omelette
Purée of broad beans
Green salad
Black cherry creams

Smoked fish mousse

Metric	Imperial	USA	
225g	8oz	8oz	smoked mackerel fillet, skinned and roughly chopped
			juice of 1 lemon
25ml	5tsp	5tsp	bottled horseradish sauce [prepared horseradish]
100g	4oz	8tbsp	butter, softened
			salt and freshly ground black pepper
150ml	¼ pint	⅔ cup	double [heavy] cream, whipped until stiff
100-g	4-oz	4-oz	can smoked oysters or mussels, drained
1	1	1	red or green pepper, cored, seeded and cut into 10 strips

Preparation time: 15 minutes plus chilling

1 Put the fish, lemon juice, horseradish and butter in a blender or food processor and blend until smooth. Taste and season with salt and pepper if necessary.
2 Fold in the whipped cream. Spoon the mousse into 6 little pots or 1 large serving bowl or dish. Chill for at least 1 hour.
3 Just before serving, garnish the top of the mousse with the smoked oysters or mussels. Put each mousse on a large plate with a few strips of pepper and slices of wholemeal [wholewheat] toast.

Asparagus omelette

Metric	Imperial	USA	
6	6	6	eggs
30ml	2tbsp	2tbsp	water
			salt and freshly ground black pepper
25g	1oz	2tbsp	butter
15ml	1tbsp	1tbsp	vegetable oil
350g	12oz	12oz	asparagus spears, fresh or frozen, cooked until tender

Preparation time: 20 minutes

1 Lightly beat the eggs with the water and season to taste with salt and pepper.
2 Heat the butter and oil in a large frying pan over a high heat. When sizzling pour in the egg mixture. Cook quickly until the omelette is set on the bottom and around the edges, but the centre still looks a little runny. (The omelette will continue to cook as you bring it to table.)
3 Working quickly, arrange the asparagus spears over one half of the omelette, with all the tips touching the edge. Fold over the other half, leaving the green tips showing.
4 Slide on to a large very hot plate and serve immediately, with purée of broad beans and green salad (see following recipes).
NOTE If cooking for only 2 or 3 people, individual omelettes look even better.

Purée of broad beans

	Metric	Imperial	USA
broad [lima] beans, fresh or frozen	700g	1½lb	1½lb
butter, melted	75g	3oz	6tbsp
salt and freshly ground black pepper			
chopped parsley, to garnish			

1 Cook the beans in boiling water until just tender. Drain well.
2 Purée the hot beans with the butter in a blender or food processor and season with salt and pepper.
3 Pile into a serving dish and sprinkle with parsley.

Preparation time: 10-15 minutes

Green salad

	Metric	Imperial	USA
a selection of salad greens – choose at least 3 varieties of lettuce such as Cos [romaine], Webb's wonder or iceberg and round [Boston or bibb], as well as watercress, mustard and cress, chicory [Belgian endive], baby raw spinach leaves and sorrel.			
chopped fresh green herbs as available (no dried ones)			
quantity of vinaigrette dressing (see page 158)	1	1	1

1 Have all the salad greens and herbs washed and thoroughly dried. At the last minute toss in the dressing.
2 Serve immediately or the leaves will wilt and lose their crisp freshness.

Preparation time: 15 minutes

Black cherry creams

	Metric	Imperial	USA
can black cherries, drained and stoned [pitted] if necessary	425-g	15-oz	16-oz
brandy, cherry brandy or maraschino liqueur	15ml	1tbsp	1tbsp
double [heavy] cream, whipped until stiff	300ml	½ pint	1¼ cups

1 Reserve 6 cherry halves to decorate; purée the remainder with the brandy in a blender or food processor.
2 Fold in the whipped cream, but not too thoroughly. It should have a slightly marbled effect.
3 Spoon into glasses and top each serving with a cherry half. Chill for at least 1 hour.

Preparation time: 10-20 minutes plus chilling

Avocado with honey and caper dressing
Chicken breasts in garlic cream sauce
Buttered broccoli with almonds
Raspberries with puff pastry hearts

Right: top left, and then clockwise:
Avocado with honey and caper dressing; Raspberries with puff pastry hearts; Chicken breasts in garlic cream sauce, with Buttered broccoli and almonds; pp91/92.

Avocado with honey and caper dressing

	Metric	Imperial	USA
vegetable oil	45ml	3tbsp	3tbsp
lemon juice	15ml	1tbsp	1tbsp
honey	15ml	1tbsp	1tbsp
capers, roughly chopped	15ml	1tbsp	1tbsp
garlic clove, peeled and crushed	1	1	1
salt and freshly ground black pepper			
ripe avocados	3	3	3

1 Combine the oil, lemon juice, honey, capers, garlic and salt and pepper to taste in a screw-topped jar. Shake well to mix.
2 Peel, halve and stone the avocados. Place each half, cut side down, on a work surface and cut across into 5mm/¼ inch thick slices. Carefully lift each half with a fish slice [slotted spatula] on to a large plate, then spread the slices a little, slightly fanning them out.
3 Pour the dressing over and serve immediately.
NOTE The dressing can be made in advance, but the avocados should ideally be cut at the last minute as they could go brown. If, however, you wish to prepare the avocados before your guests arrive, brush thoroughly with lemon juice to prevent discoloration.

Preparation time: 15-20 minutes

Chicken breasts in garlic cream sauce

	Metric	Imperial	USA
butter	15g	½oz	1tbsp
vegetable oil	15ml	1tbsp	1tbsp
small onion, peeled and very finely chopped	½	½	½
garlic cloves, peeled and crushed	4	4	4
double [heavy] cream	300ml	½ pint	1¼ cups
salt and freshly ground black pepper			
skinned chicken breasts [chicken breast halves]	6	6	6

1 Heat the butter and oil in a large pan (a sauté pan is ideal) and cook the onion until transparent. Add the garlic and cream and season with salt and pepper. Bring to the boil, stirring, then turn down the heat to very low.
2 Place the chicken breasts in the pan, in one layer if possible. Cover and cook over a low heat for 10 minutes, turning once. Check the chicken is cooked through, but do not overcook.
3 Transfer the chicken to hot plates and coat with the garlic cream sauce. Serve with buttered broccoli with almonds (see following recipe).

Preparation time: 25 minutes

Buttered broccoli with almonds

Metric	Imperial	USA	
700g	1½lb	1½lb	broccoli spears
50g	2oz	4tbsp	butter
1	1	1	garlic clove, peeled and crushed
50g	2oz	½ cup	flaked [slivered] almonds
			salt and freshly ground black pepper

Preparation time: 10-15 minutes

1 Steam the broccoli until just tender.

2 Meanwhile, melt the butter in a large saucepan and cook the garlic and almonds for 30 seconds, stirring. Do not let the butter brown.

3 Add the broccoli to the pan and toss till coated with the butter and almonds. Season with salt and pepper and serve hot.

Raspberries with puff pastry hearts

Metric	Imperial	USA	
225g	8oz	8oz	puff pastry, thawed if frozen
1	1	1	egg, mixed with a little milk, to glaze
			sugar
150ml	¼ pint	⅔ cup	single [light] cream
350g	12oz	12oz	raspberries, thawed if frozen
32	32	32	mint leaves or rose petals

Oven temperature: 220°C/ 425°F/Gas Mark 7
Preparation time: 40 minutes plus cooling

1 Roll out the pastry very thinly and cut out 18 small heart shapes, or small diamonds if you have no heart-shaped cutter. Place on a dampened baking sheet. Brush with the egg and milk glaze and sprinkle with a little sugar.

2 Bake in the oven for about 15 minutes or until puffed and golden. Cool.

3 To assemble, spoon a little cream into the centre of each of 6 large flat plates. Divide the fruit equally and make a little island in the middle of each pool of cream. Arrange 4 pastry hearts around the 'islands' alternating with 4 mint leaves or rose petals.

NOTE In winter crystallised rose petals could be substituted or leaves or petals omitted completely. The cream can also be omitted if you feel it is too sinful to have cream twice in one meal.

Smoked mackerel fillet with two sauces
Three pasta shapes with poppy seeds and butter
Carrot and orange salad
Melon in green ginger wine

Smoked mackerel fillet with two sauces

	Metric	Imperial	USA
small smoked mackerel fillets, or 3 large ones cut in half lengthways	6	6	6
pickled walnuts, sliced	6	6	6
Sauce one			
single [light] cream	30ml	2tbsp	2tbsp
mayonnaise	60ml	4tbsp	¼ cup
horseradish relish to taste			
Sauce two			
sour cream	90ml	6tbsp	6tbsp
bunch watercress, washed and picked over	½	½	½

1 Combine the ingredients of sauce one. To make sauce two, put the sour cream and watercress in a blender or food processor and process till smooth and pale green.

2 Place 15ml/1tbsp of each sauce on opposite sides of each plate. Arrange a fish fillet along the line made where the two sauces join. Place the pickled walnut slices down the centre of the mackerel.

NOTE You will probably not need to salt the sauces as the fish already contains suficient.

Preparation time: 20 minutes

Three pasta shapes with poppy seeds and butter

	Metric	Imperial	USA
dried pasta, 175g/6oz of each of 3 different shapes	500g	18oz	18oz
butter	175g	6oz	12tbsp
garlic cloves, peeled and cut into quarters	3	3	3
poppy seeds	30ml	2tbsp	2tbsp
salt and freshly ground black pepper			

1 Cook the pasta according to the instructions on the packet.

2 Meanwhile, melt the butter in a small saucepan over a very low heat. Add the garlic pieces and cook, stirring occasionally, for 2-3 minutes or

Preparation time: 15-20 minutes

until the garlic has flavoured the butter. Do not allow the butter to brown. Remove the garlic with a slotted spoon and discard.

3 Place the poppy seeds on a piece of foil and cook under a preheated grill [broiler] for 2-3 minutes or until they smell toasted. Tip into the garlic-flavoured butter. Add salt and pepper to taste.

4 Drain the pasta and mix the different shapes together. Pour the butter and poppy seed mixture over the pasta, toss to coat evenly and serve immediately, in hot bowls or on hot plates.

Below: Smoked mackerel fillet with two sauces; p93.

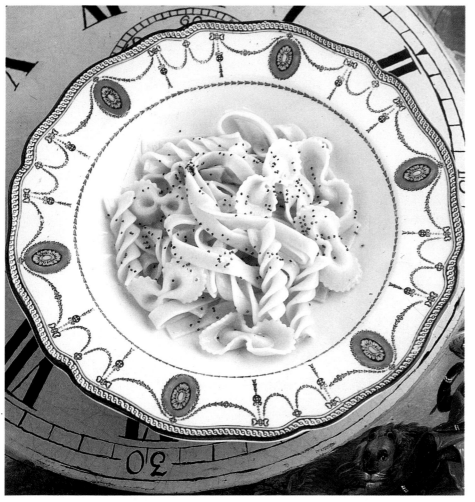

Left: Three pasta shapes with poppy seeds and butter; p93.

Carrot and orange salad

	Metric	Imperial	USA
grated rind and juice of ½ small orange			
olive oil	45ml	3tbsp	3tbsp
garlic clove, peeled and chopped	1	1	1
salt and freshly ground black pepper			
carrots, scraped and grated	275g	10oz	2½ cups
chopped parsley, to garnish			

1 Make a dressing with the orange rind and juice, olive oil, garlic, and salt and pepper to taste.

2 About 30 minutes before serving, toss the grated carrot in the dressing. Sprinkle with chopped parsley.

Preparation time: 15 minutes plus marinating

Melon in green ginger wine

Metric	Imperial	USA	
1	1	1	ripe melon such as ogen, cantalaloupe, honeydew, etc. (type in season)
175ml	6floz	¾ cup	green ginger wine (or more if preferred)
			lightly whipped cream
6	6	6	pieces of preserved stem ginger in syrup, quartered (optional)

Preparation time: 15 minutes plus chilling

1 Peel the melon and discard the seeds. Cut into cubes or balls. Place in a bowl, pour over the green ginger wine and stir. Cover closely and chill for at least 1 hour.

2 To serve, spoon the melon and juices into glasses or bowls and garnish with whipped cream and pieces of preserved ginger, if used.

Palm hearts in sour cream
Cornish fisherman's pasties
Hot lettuce and peas
Exotic fruit salad

Palm hearts in sour cream

Metric	Imperial	USA	
2 225-g	2 8-oz	2 8-oz	cans palm hearts, drained and cut crossways into thin slices
150ml	¼ pint	⅔ cup	sour cream
3	3	3	spring onions [scallions], trimmed and sliced
25g	1oz	¼ cup	Parmesan cheese, freshly grated
			freshly ground black pepper

Preparation time: 15 minutes

Arrange the slices of palm heart on 6 plates. Spoon over the cream and sprinkle over the onions, Parmesan and a twist of black pepper.

Cornish fisherman's pasties

Metric	Imperial	USA	
100g	4oz	1 cup	cucumber, finely diced
			salt and freshly ground black pepper
30ml	2tbsp	2tbsp	double [heavy] cream
100g	4oz	4oz	cream cheese
450g	1lb	1lb	puff pastry, thawed if frozen
175g	6oz	6oz	cooked fresh salmon fillet, skin removed and flaked
1	1	1	egg yolk, mixed with a little milk

1 Sprinkle the cucumber with a little salt and leave to drain in a colander for 1 hour. Rinse and dry on paper towels.

2 Work the cream into the cheese, adding salt and pepper to taste.

3 Roll out the pastry thinly. Using the top of an 18cm/7 inch bowl as a guide, cut out 6 rounds.

4 Leaving a border clear, divide the cheese mixture between the 6 pastry rounds. Pile the flaked salmon and cucumber on top, to make neat little mounds.

5 Thoroughly dampen the pastry borders, then fold each round in half over the filling to make half moon shapes. Seal the edges well with a fork, pressing in little ridges all the way round to make a decorative edge.

6 Now turn each little parcel so that the flat part is underneath. Flute the upstanding 'seams' so the finished pies look like Cornish pasties.

7 Brush each little pasty with the egg yolk glaze and place on a dampened baking sheet. Bake at the top of the oven for about 20 minutes or until crisp and evenly golden. After about 7 or 8 minutes cooking time, prick each pie in a couple of places with a small skewer or darning needle to release any steam.

8 Serve with hot lettuce and peas (see following recipe).

Oven temperature: 220°C/ 425°F/Gas Mark 7
Preparation time: 45 minutes plus draining

Hot lettuce and peas

	Metric	Imperial	USA
iceberg or Cos [romaine] lettuce, roughly chopped	350g	12oz	6 cups
shelled peas	225g	8oz	2 cups
butter, melted	50g	2oz	4tbsp
salt and freshly ground black pepper			

1 Steam the lettuce and peas for about 5 minutes or until just tender.

2 Toss the vegetables in the melted butter and season with salt and pepper. Serve hot.

Preparation time: 10 minutes

Exotic fruit salad

	Metric	Imperial	USA
can guava halves	425-g	15-oz	16-oz
can sliced mangoes	425-g	15-oz	16-oz
can lychees	425-g	15-oz	16-oz
rum, brandy or liqueur of your choice (optional)	15ml	1tbsp	1tbsp

Mix together the fruits and their syrup. Stir in the alcohol, if used.

Preparation time: 10 minutes

Right: Palm hearts in sour cream; p96.

Left: Exotic fruit salad; p97.

Globe artichokes with pesto mayonnaise
Warm kipper-stuffed croissants
Whisked horseradish cream sauce
Gingered carrots
Salad of two cresses
Irish coffee jelly

Left: Globe artichokes with pesto mayonnaise; p100.

Right: Warm kipper-stuffed croissants with Gingered carrots and Salad of two cresses; p100/101.

Globe artichokes with pesto mayonnaise

Metric	Imperial	USA	
6	6	6	globe artichokes
200ml	7fl oz	1 cup	mayonnaise (see page 158)
20ml	4tsp	5tsp	pesto sauce, bought ready made
			fresh basil leaves, if available

Preparation time: 1 hour plus cooling

1 Cut the stems off the artichokes, level with the base. Cook in plenty of boiling salted water in a covered pan for 45 minutes or until one of the bottom leaves can be pulled away easily. Drain and cool, upside-down, to room temperature.
2 Mix the mayonnaise with the pesto.
3 To serve, place an artichoke on each plate with some of the pesto mayonnaise spooned next to it. Garnish the plate with basil leaves if available.
NOTE Don't forget to provide bowls or one communal bowl in which to place discarded leaves.

Warm kipper-stuffed croissants

Metric	Imperial	USA	
3	3	3	fresh croissants
3	3	3	kipper fillets, skinned and halved lengthways

Oven temperature: 140°C/ 275°F/Gas Mark 1
Preparation time: 15 minutes

1 Heat the croissants in the oven for about 10 minutes. When really hot, split open.
2 Meanwhile, cook the kippers under a preheated grill [broiler] for about 5 minutes or until really hot.
3 To serve, place a croissant bottom on each of 6 large hot plates and lay a piece of kipper fillet across this. Replace the croissant 'lid' and serve hot, with whisked horseradish cream sauce and gingered carrots (see following recipes).

Whisked horseradish cream sauce

Metric	Imperial	USA	
175ml	6fl oz	¾ cup	double [heavy] cream
20ml	4tsp	4tsp	bottled horseradish sauce [prepared horseradish]

Whip the cream until foamy and thick but not stiff. Gently whisk in the horseradish sauce.

Gingered carrots

	Metric	Imperial	USA
carrots, scraped and cut into 5mm/¼ inch sticks	450g	1lb	1lb
butter	50g	2oz	4tbsp
vegetable oil	15ml	1tbsp	1tbsp
cube fresh ginger, peeled and finely chopped	2.5-cm	1-inch	1-inch
salt and freshly ground black pepper			
chopped parsley, to garnish			

1 Place the carrots in a saucepan with the butter, oil and ginger. Season with salt and pepper. Cover and cook over a very gentle heat, shaking the pan occasionally, for 10-15 minutes or until the carrots are just tender.
2 Sprinkle with chopped parsley and serve hot.

Preparation time: 20-25 minutes

Salad of two cresses

	Metric	Imperial	USA
bunch watercress, washed and picked over	1	1	1
box mustard and cress [garden cress or alfalfa sprouts], cut from box	1	1	1
quantity vinaigrette dressing (see page 158)	1	1	1

Mix the 2 cresses together and toss with the dressing at the last minute.

Preparation time: 5 minutes

Irish coffee jelly

	Metric	Imperial	USA
freshly made black coffee	1.2 litres	2 pints	5 cups
unflavoured gelatine	2 sachets	2 sachets	2½ env.
Irish whiskey	30ml	2tbsp	2tbsp
sugar			
single [light] cream (or more as liked)	150ml	¼ pint	⅔ cup

1 Pour 300ml/½ pint [1¼ cups] of coffee into a saucepan and sprinkle over the gelatine. Heat gently, stirring, until completely dissolved. Add the gelatine mixture to the rest of the coffee. Mix in the whiskey and sweeten to taste.
2 Pour into 6 glasses. Leave to set in the refrigerator for at least 6 hours.
3 Just before serving, pour the cream over the tops of the jellies.
NOTE This dessert should be sweetened with a certain amount of sugar, even when serving to guests who would not normally take sugar in coffee.

Preparation time: 10 minutes plus chilling

THINNER DINNERS

Right: top left, and then clockwise:
Ricotta and anchovy pâté; Steamed turkey breast, threaded with sweet peppers and Broad bean, wheat and onion salad; Minted cucumber and yogurt soup; Jellied fruit terrine; pp104-106.

AL FRESCO FAYRE   Party menu for 12 people
Minted cucumber and yogurt soup
Ricotta and anchovy pâté
Steamed turkey breast, threaded with sweet peppers
Broad bean, wheat and onion salad
Jellied fruit terrine

Minted cucumber and yogurt soup

Metric	Imperial	USA	
3.6 litres	6 pints	15 cups	chicken or vegetable stock (see page 156)
900ml	1½ pints	3¾ cups	plain low-fat yogurt
1	1	1	large cucumber, roughly chopped
2	2	2	garlic cloves, peeled and crushed
45ml	3tbsp	3tbsp	chopped fresh mint (or more to taste)
			salt and freshly ground black pepper
			mint leaves and cucumber slices, to garnish

Preparation time: 10 minutes plus chilling

1 Place the stock, yogurt, cucumber and garlic in a blender or food processor and blend till smooth (work in manageable batches). Stir in the chopped mint and season to taste with salt and pepper. Chill for at least 2 hours.
2 To serve, pour into chilled soup bowls and garnish with mint leaves and cucumber slices.

Ricotta and anchovy pâté

Metric	Imperial	USA	
900g	2lb	2lb	ricotta cheese
150g	5oz	5oz	canned anchovy fillets, drained and roughly chopped
22.5-30ml	1½-2tbsp	1½-2tbsp	lemon juice
			freshly ground black pepper
			fresh herbs, as available, to garnish
			lemon wedges, to serve

Preparation time: 10 minutes plus chilling

1 Blend the cheese with the anchovies and lemon juice in a blender or food processor until well amalgamated and smooth. Season with pepper to taste.
2 Spoon the pâté into a bowl or serving dish and chill for at least 1 hour.
3 To serve, garnish with fresh herbs and serve with lemon wedges and bran crackers or other plain savoury biscuits [crackers].

Steamed turkey breast, threaded with sweet peppers

	Metric	Imperial	USA
boneless turkey breast roasts, thawed if frozen	2 550-g	2 1¼-lb	2 1¼-lb
red pepper, cored, seeded and cut into 5mm/¼ inch strips	1	1	1
green pepper, cored, seeded and cut into 5mm/¼ inch strips	1	1	1

1 Remove the outer wrapper from the meat, but leave on the inner one which keeps the meat in shape during cooking.

2 Using a larding needle, thread strips of red and green pepper through the meat from top to bottom, trimming the strips level with the top and bottom of the roast. (This is best done with a pair of scissors.)

3 Stand the roasts on lightly oiled saucers and arrange in steamers. Steam for 1 hour.

4 Allow to cool, then remove the wrapper and any fat from around the outside of the meat. Slice thinly for serving.

NOTE Threading the meat with the pepper strips is much quicker and easier than it sounds and is best done when the meat has just thawed, so that the roast is still quite cold and firm.

Preparation time: 1½ hours plus cooling

Broad bean, wheat and onion salad

	Metric	Imperial	USA
whole wheat kernels	225g	8oz	1¾ cups
broad [or lima] beans, cooked and cooled	450g	1lb	1lb
spring onions [scallions], trimmed and sliced	6	6	6
lemon juice	15ml	1tbsp	1tbsp
olive oil	15ml	1tbsp	1tbsp
garlic clove, peeled and crushed	1	1	1
salt and freshly ground black pepper			
chopped parsley, to garnish			

1 Cook the wheat in boiling water (without salt) for 1 hour. Drain and cool.

2 Mix the wheat in a serving bowl with the broad beans and onions.

3 Make a dressing with the lemon juice, oil and garlic and season with salt and pepper. Pour over the salad and toss. Sprinkle with parsley.

NOTE This salad is best dressed about 1 hour before serving and eaten at room temperature.

Preparation time: 1¼ hours plus marinating

Jellied fruit terrine

(Make 2 to serve 12)

Metric	Imperial	USA	
600ml	1 pint	2½ cups	clear apple juice or white grape juice
2 packets	2 packets	1½ env.	unflavoured gelatine
1	1	1	small orange, peeled and sliced crossways
100g	4oz	4oz	seedless grapes
1	1	1	banana, peeled and sliced

Preparation time: 30 minutes plus cooling and chilling

1 Heat 150ml/5fl oz [⅔ cup] of the fruit juice in a small pan. Sprinkle on the gelatine and heat gently, stirring constantly, until all the gelatine is dissolved. Do not boil.

2 Return the gelatine mixture to the rest of the fruit juice and allow to cool.

3 Pour a 5mm/¼ inch layer of the jelly mixture into the bottom of a dampened small loaf tin with a capacity of 900ml/1½ pints [1 quart]. Chill until the jelly is almost set.

4 Arrange slices of orange on the almost-set jelly layer and pour over more liquid jelly, just to cover the orange. Chill until set.

5 Repeat this process, using the grapes and banana slices (do not slice the banana until the last minute or it will go black). Finish with a layer of jelly. This is a very firm jelly mixture, as it needs to support the fruit. If it should begin to set too soon before the terrine is completed, stand the container holding the liquid jelly in a bowl of hot water. Chill until firmly set – at least 4 hours.

6 Dip the tin briefly in hot water and turn out the jellied terrine on to a flat plate. Slice carefully with a very sharp knife.

NOTE Fruit can be varied according to preference. All strawberry slices in grape juice, for instance, would be delicious.

Right: Cucumber mousse; p108.

Cucumber mousse
Ribbons of plaice, steamed in leaves
Hot root and fruit salad
Gingered rhubarb in orange

Cucumber mousse

Metric	Imperial	USA	
150ml	¼ pint	⅔ cup	chicken or vegetable stock (see page 156)
1 sachet	1 sachet	1 env.	unflavoured gelatine
120ml	4fl oz	½ cup	plain low fat yogurt
175g	6oz	1½ cups	cucumber, roughly chopped
175g	6oz	6oz	silken tofu (beancurd)
1	1	1	garlic clove, peeled and crushed
10ml	2tsp	2tsp	lemon juice
			salt and pepper
2	2	2	egg whites, beaten until stiff
			thin cucumber slices

Preparation time: 30 minutes
plus chilling

1 Heat the stock in a small saucepan. Sprinkle on the gelatine and heat gently, stirring, until all the gelatine is dissolved. Do not boil.

2 Pour the gelatine mixture into a blender or food processor and add the yogurt, chopped cucumber, tofu, garlic, lemon juice and salt and pepper to taste. Blend until smooth.

3 Tip into a bowl and fold in the beaten egg whites. Place a cucumber slice in the bottom of 6 dampened ramekins or other moulds, then pour in the mixture. Chill until set — at least 3 hours.

4 To turn out, run a small sharp knife round the outside of each mousse, dip the moulds into hot water for a few seconds and turn out on to 6 plates. Garnish with halved cucumber slices.

Ribbons of plaice, steamed in leaves

	Metric	Imperial	USA
large cabbage leaves	6	6	6
tomatoes, skinned, seeded and finely diced	350g	12oz	3 cups
plaice [flounder] fillet, skinned and cut into 1cm/½ inch strips diagonally	700g	1½lb	1½lb
chopped parsley	30ml	2tbsp	2tbsp
salt and freshly ground black pepper			
lemon juice			
fresh basil leaves, if available	6	6	6

1 Trim down the thick central stem of each cabbage leaf with a sharp knife so that it is the same thickness as the rest of the leaf. Blanch in boiling water for 3-4 minutes or until softened. Rinse in cold water to stop cooking and pat dry with paper towels.

Preparation time: 45 minutes

2 Lay the leaves out flat in front of you. Divide half the tomato dice between the leaves, making a little pile in the centre. Divide the fish strips between the leaves, mounding them on top of the tomatoes. Cover this with the rest of the tomato. Sprinkle over the parsley and season with salt, pepper and lemon juice. Lay a basil leaf on top if used.

3 Bring up the sides of each leaf, then fold over the top and bottom to enclose the filling and make a neat parcel. Secure each parcel with 1 or 2 wooden cocktail sticks.

4 Arrange the parcels on a lightly oiled plate (or saucers) in a steamer and steam for 10 minutes.

5 To serve, take out the cocktail sticks and place the opened parcels on 6 hot plates. Serve with hot root and fruit salad (see following recipe).

Hot root and fruit salad

Metric	Imperial	USA	
175g	6oz	6oz	parsnip, peeled and cut into small sticks
175g	6oz	6oz	turnip, peeled and cut into small sticks
175g	6oz	6oz	swede [rutabaga], peeled and cut into small sticks
175g	6oz	6oz	carrot, scraped and cut into small sticks
22.5ml	1½tbsp	1½tbsp	olive oil
15ml	1tbsp	1tbsp	lemon juice
1	1	1	garlic clove, peeled and crushed
600ml	1 pint	2½ cups	unsweetened orange juice
			salt and freshly ground black pepper
			chopped parsley, to garnish

Preparation time: 35-45 minutes

1 Place all the ingredients in a saucepan. Bring to the boil, cover and simmer over a low heat for 7-10 minutes or until the vegetables are just tender.
2 Spoon the vegetables and juice on to each plate and sprinkle with parsley.

Gingered rhubarb in orange

Metric	Imperial	USA	
700g	1½lb	1½lb	rhubarb, cut into 2.5cm/1 inch pieces
30ml	2tbsp	2tbsp	sugar
10ml	2tsp	2tsp	ground ginger
300ml	½ pint	1¼ cups	orange juice
6	6	6	pieces preserved ginger in syrup, quartered (optional)

Preparation time: 20 minutes plus chilling

1 Place the rhubarb in a large saucepan with the sugar and ground ginger. Pour over the orange juice. Bring to the boil, then cover and cook gently for 2-3 minutes or until the rhubarb is just tender, but still in pieces and not turned to mush. (This can happen so quickly, that it is best to stand by the pan the whole time.)
2 Pour into a serving bowl or into individual glasses or bowls. Garnish with a few pieces of stem ginger (if used) and chill.
NOTE Try to buy sticks of rhubarb of uniform thickness, so that they will all cook in the same time.

Right: top: Pomander chicken with poached pears in green peppercorn sauce; **below:** Aubergine [eggplant] pâté; p112.

Aubergine pâté
Pomander chicken, with poached pears in green peppercorn sauce
Three fruit sorbet

Aubergine pâté

Metric	Imperial	USA	
450g	1lb	1lb	aubergines [eggplants]
2	2	2	slices wholemeal [wholewheat] bread
7.5ml	½tbsp	½tbsp	olive oil
1	1	1	small onion, peeled and chopped
1	1	1	garlic clove, peeled and crushed
15ml	1tbsp	1tbsp	chopped parsley
15ml	1tbsp	1tbsp	plain low-fat yogurt
10ml	2tsp	2tsp	lemon juice
			salt and freshly ground black pepper
			parsley, to garnish

Oven temperature: 220°C/ 425°F/Gas Mark 7
Preparation time: 1¼ hours plus cooling and chilling

1 Prick the aubergines all over with a fork and bake in the oven until soft. Cool, then split open and scoop out all the flesh. Discard the skin.
2 Place the bread in a blender or food processor and make small crumbs.
3 Heat the oil in a small pan and cook the onion until golden brown. Tip the cooked onion into the blender or food processor with the bread-crumbs and add the aubergine flesh, garlic, parsley, yogurt and lemon juice. Season with salt and pepper. Blend until smooth.
4 Spoon into serving dishes and chill. Serve garnished with parsley, with wholemeal [wholewheat] or white pitta bread.

Pomander chicken, with poached pears in green peppercorn sauce

Metric	Imperial	USA	
7.5ml	½tbsp	½tbsp	vegetable oil
1	1	1	small onion, peeled and chopped
175ml	6fl oz	¾ cup	white wine
250ml	8fl oz	1 cup	chicken or vegetable stock (see page 156)
			pared rind of ½ small orange, cut into long thin slivers
3	3	3	hard pears, peeled, cored and cut into long thin slices
			salt and freshly ground black pepper
18	18	18	whole cloves
6	6	6	chicken breast fillets
20ml	4tsp	4tsp	arrowroot, dissolved in a little water
10ml	2tsp	2tsp	green peppercorns

1 In a large pan (a sauté pan is ideal) big enough to accommodate the chicken breasts in one layer, heat the oil over a low heat and cook the onion until transparent. Be careful not to let the onion burn. Add the wine, stock, orange rind, pear slices and salt and pepper to taste. Bring to the boil, cover and simmer over low heat until the pears are tender. (This could take up to 40 minutes – the time will depend on the type of pear.) With a slotted spoon, remove the pear slices to a heated dish, cover and keep warm.

2 Push 3 whole cloves into the top of each chicken breast and arrange in one layer in the liquid in the pan. Cover and cook over low heat for 10 minutes.

3 Using a slotted spoon, remove the chicken to the dish with the pears. Cover and keep warm.

4 Add the dissolved arrowroot and peppercorns to the sauce and heat gently, stirring, until slightly thickened.

5 To serve, place a chicken breast and some slices of pear on each of 6 heated plates and pour over sauce.

NOTE The cloves should not be eaten; however, they do look pretty in the finished dish, so if you decide to leave them in for serving, don't forget to tell your guests to remove them.

Preparation time: 1¼ hours

Three fruit sorbet

	Metric	Imperial	USA
apple juice	450ml	¾ pint	2 cups
orange juice	450ml	¾ pint	2 cups
grape juice	450ml	¾ pint	2 cups
fresh fruit slices			
mint leaves (optional)			

1 Pour the juices into 3 separate shallow containers and freeze till slushy. Take out and mash well with a fork to break up any ice crystals, then freeze again.

2 Remove from the freezer to the refrigerator 1 hour before required.

3 To serve, arrange a spoonful of each sorbet on each plate and garnish with fruit slices and mint leaves (if used).

Preparation time: 10 minutes plus freezing

Clear fish and vegetable soup
Sea shells
Shred salad
Limey jelly

Left: Clear fish and vegetable soup; p115.

Left: Sea shells; p116.

Clear fish and vegetable soup

	Metric	Imperial	USA
swede [rutabaga], peeled and cut into 3mm/⅛ inch thick slices	100g	4oz	4oz
spring onions [scallions], trimmed and cut into julienne strips	2	2	2
asparagus spears, cut in half crossways	6	6	6
thin slices bulb fennel	6	6	6
broad [or lima] beans	18	18	18
chicken or vegetable stock (see page 156)	1.8 litres	3 pints	7½ cups
mussels, scrubbed and cleaned (see page 9)	18	18	18
cooked prawns [shrimp], shelled and thawed if frozen	100g	4oz	4oz
skinless plaice [flounder] fillet, cut into 5mm/¼ inch strips crossways	100g	4oz	4oz
chopped parsley, to garnish			

1 With a decorative small cutter, cut shapes (ie small hearts) from the swede slices. Place these, with the onions, asparagus, fennel and broad beans in a large saucepan. Pour on the stock, bring to the boil and simmer for 5 minutes or until the swede is just tender.

2 Add the mussels, prawns and plaice and continue to cook only until all the mussels have opened. By this time the plaice will be cooked and the prawns heated through. Do not cook any longer.

3 Pour into 6 heated bowls, making sure that everyone has an equal portion of all ingredients. Sprinkle with a little parsley and serve immediately.

Preparation time: 25-30 minutes

Sea shells

Metric	Imperial	USA	
30	30	30	large pasta shells (about 225g/8oz)
7.5ml	½tbsp	½tbsp	olive oil
1	1	1	small onion, peeled and chopped
1	1	1	garlic clove, peeled and crushed
2.5ml	½tsp	½tsp	dried oregano
600ml	1 pint	2½ cups	pure tomato juice
25ml	5tsp	5tsp	lemon juice
			salt and freshly ground black pepper
50g	2oz	1 cup	fresh brown breadcrumbs
45ml	3tbsp	3tbsp	finely chopped parsley
175g	6oz	6oz	white crabmeat, drained if canned, thawed if frozen
175g	6oz	6oz	ricotta cheese, mashed

Oven temperature: 160°C/
325°F/Gas Mark 3
Preparation time: 1¼ hours

1 Cook the pasta in plenty of boiling water for about 12 minutes or until just tender. When ready, drain and cool.

2 Meanwhile, make the sauce. Heat the oil in a saucepan and cook the onion until transparent. Add the garlic, oregano, tomato juice, 10ml/2tsp lemon juice and salt and pepper to taste. Bring to the boil, then cover and simmer for 5 minutes.

3 Make the stuffing by mixing together the breadcrumbs, parsley, crabmeat, remaining lemon juice and ricotta and season with salt and pepper.

4 Stuff the pasta shells with this mixture.

5 Pour the tomato sauce into a shallow baking dish that will just hold the pasta shells snugly in one layer. Arrange the shells, stuffing side up, on top of the sauce.

6 Cover the dish and cook in the oven for 30 minutes.

7 Remove the shells to a warm plate or dish. Divide the sauce between 6 hot plates and arrange 5 shells on each plate, in a starfish shape. Serve immediately.

Shred salad

	Metric	Imperial	USA
carrot, scraped and cut into long thin strips	175g	6oz	1½ cups
Cos [romaine] lettuce or chinese leaves [Nappa or celery cabbage], cut into long strips	175g	6oz	3 cups
spring onions [scallions], trimmed and cut into long thin strips	3	3	3
quantity vinaigrette dressing (see page 158)	1	1	1
chives, cut into 8cm/3 inch lengths			

Mix together the carrot, lettuce and onion 'shreds'. Pour over the dressing and toss to coat evenly. Scatter chives on top and serve.
NOTE If on a strict diet, dress the salad with lemon juice only.

Preparation time: 15 minutes

Limey jelly

	Metric	Imperial	USA
juice of 4 limes, made up to 600ml/1 pint [2½ cups] with boiling water			
sugar	30ml	2tbsp	2tbsp
unflavoured gelatine	1½ sachet	1½ sachet	2 env.

1 Stir the lime liquid with the sugar until the sugar has dissolved. Heat half the lime liquid in a small pan and sprinkle on the gelatine. Stir over low heat until dissolved, then add the remaining liquid. Pour into a dampened 600ml/1 pint [3 cup] mould and chill until set.
2 To serve, dip the mould briefly in hot water and turn out on to a serving plate.
NOTE If you prefer softer jelly, or are nervous of turning a jelly out, use only 1 sachet [1 env.] gelatine and pour into 6 small pretty glasses or dishes for setting. Serve in the glasses.

Preparation time: 10 minutes plus chilling

Left: Shred salad; p117.
Below: Limey jelly; p117.

Chilled uncooked tomato soup
Pesto sorbet
Seafood fricassée
Leaf parcels
Winter, summer pudding

Chilled uncooked tomato soup

	Metric	Imperial	USA
tomatoes, roughly chopped	700g	1½lb	1½lb
garlic cloves, peeled and crushed	2	2	2
spring onions [scallions], peeled and roughly chopped	3	3	3
sugar	10ml	2tsp	2tsp
dash of Worcestershire sauce (optional)			
lemon juice	10ml	2tsp	2tsp
concentrated tomato purée [paste]	30ml	2tbsp	2tbsp
salt and freshly ground black pepper			
chicken or vegetable stock (see page 156)	1.5 litres	2½ pints	6¼ cups

1 Purée all the ingredients except the stock together in a blender or food processor. Strain through a fine sieve into a bowl. Discard the solids in the sieve.
2 Add the cold stock and chill the soup.
3 Serve in chilled bowls, with a dollop of pesto sorbet (see following recipe) in the centre of each.

Preparation time: 10 minutes plus chilling

Pesto sorbet

	Metric	Imperial	USA
chicken or vegetable stock (see page 156)	600ml	1 pint	2½ cups
pesto sauce, bought ready made	25ml	5tsp	5tsp

1 Blend the ingredients together in a blender or food processor.
2 Pour the mixture into a shallow container and freeze till slushy. Take out and mash well with a fork to break up any ice crystals, then freeze again.
3 Remove from the freezer to the refrigerator 1 hour before required.

Preparation time: 10 minutes plus freezing

Seafood fricassée

Metric	Imperial	USA	
15ml	1tbsp	1tbsp	vegetable oil
1	1	1	small onion, peeled and chopped
225g	8oz	8oz	salmon fillet, skinned and cubed
225g	8oz	8oz	monkfish tail, cubed
225g	8oz	8oz	scallops, sliced
225g	8oz	8oz	peeled cooked prawns [shrimp], thawed if frozen
			salt and freshly ground black pepper
10ml	2tsp	2tsp	capers, roughly chopped
120ml	4fl oz	½ cup	dry white vermouth
			chopped parsley or dill, to garnish
			lemon wedges, to serve

Preparation time: 25 minutes

1 Heat the oil in a frying pan and cook the onion until transparent over a medium heat.

2 Add the salmon and monkfish and stir-fry for 1 minute. Add the scallops and prawns, season with salt and pepper and cook 1 minute more.

3 Stir in the capers and vermouth and bring to the boil. Simmer, stirring gently so as not to break the fish pieces, for 1-2 minutes or until there is hardly any liquid left, merely a glaze.

4 Spoon the seafood on to 6 heated plates and sprinkle with parsley or dill. Arrange two leaf parcels (see following recipe) on each plate and garnish the plate with lemon wedges.

Leaf parcels

Metric	Imperial	USA	
12	12	12	large cabbage leaves, about 15cm/6 inches across
15ml	1tbsp	1tbsp	olive oil
2	2	2	spring onions [scallions], trimmed and chopped
50g	2oz	½ cup	mushrooms, wiped and chopped
1	1	1	garlic clove, peeled and crushed
100g	4oz	⅔ cup	cooked rice
25g	1oz	½ cup	fresh brown breadcrumbs
			pinch of dried thyme
			salt and freshly ground black pepper
1	1	1	egg, beaten

Preparation time: 45 minutes

1 Trim the stalks of each leaf level with the rest of the leaf. Blanch the leaves in boiling salted water for 3-5 minutes or until tender. Drain and refresh in cold water. Drain again and pat dry on paper towels.

2 Heat the oil in a small saucepan and cook the onions for 2 minutes. Add the mushrooms and garlic, cover and cook over a low heat, shaking the pan occasionally, for 5 minutes.

3 Tip the vegetables into a bowl and mix well with the rice and breadcrumbs. Season with thyme, salt and pepper and bind with the beaten egg.

4 Divide this stuffing between the cabbage leaves, making a neat pile in the centre of each. Fold up the sides of each leaf over the filling and then fold over the top and bottom. Place these parcels seam side down on an oiled plate or plates. Arrange in a steamer and steam for 15 minutes. Serve hot.

Winter, summer pudding

	Metric	Imperial	USA
firm pears, peeled, cored and sliced	350g	12oz	12oz
sweet apples, peeled, cored and sliced	225g	8oz	8oz
dried apricots, soaked, drained and halved	50g	2oz	½ cup
apple juice	350ml	12fl oz	1½ cups
small sliced white loaf, crusts removed	1	1	1

1 Place the fruit in a saucepan with the apple juice. Cover and simmer just until the fruit is tender. Cool.

2 Line a 1.2 litre/2 pint [5-cup] pudding bowl or mould with the bread, overlapping the slices very slightly and cutting to shape.

3 Pour half the fruit and cooking juices into the lined bowl. Lay a slice of bread on top and fill the bowl with the rest of the fruit. Cover the top with more bread. Place a small plate or saucer, which fits exactly inside the top of the bowl, on top of the pudding. Place a weight or cans of food on top. Chill for at least 4 hours, preferably 6-8.

4 To serve, turn out the pudding and slice.

NOTE This is, of course, delicious served with cream, but for the weight-conscious, plain low-fat yogurt is almost as good.

Preparation time: 45 minutes plus soaking and chilling

Below: Chilled uncooked tomato soup with Pesto sorbet; p119.

Left: top: Parsnip and garlic soufflé with Cooked orange sauce; **centre:** Ratatouille niçoise, **below:** Ricotta cheese and fresh fruit; pp123–125.

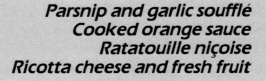

Parsnip and garlic soufflé
Cooked orange sauce
Ratatouille niçoise
Ricotta cheese and fresh fruit

Parsnip and garlic soufflé

	Metric	Imperial	USA
parsnips, peeled and sliced	350g	12oz	12oz
garlic cloves, peeled but left whole	6	6	6
butter	25g	1oz	2tbsp
flour	25g	1oz	3tbsp
milk	450ml	¾ pint	2 cups
eggs, separated	6	6	6
salt and white pepper			

1 Cook the parsnips with the whole garlic cloves in boiling salted water until the parsnips are tender. Drain and mash or purée the parsnips and garlic in a blender or food processor.

Oven temperature: 200°C/ 400°F/Gas Mark 6
Preparation time: 1¼ hours

2 Melt the butter in a saucepan and add the flour. Cook over medium heat, stirring, for 2-3 minutes. Add the milk and bring to the boil slowly, stirring constantly to avoid lumps forming. Simmer for 2-3 minutes until you have a nice thick sauce.

3 Remove the pan from the heat and gradually beat in the egg yolks. Mix in the parsnip purée and season generously with salt and pepper.

4 Beat the egg whites with a pinch of salt until stiff. Fold into the mixture. Spoon into a buttered and floured 2 litres/3 pint/7 cup soufflé dish. Bake in the oven for 30-40 minutes.

5 Serve immediately with cooked orange sauce (see following recipe).

NOTE 30 minutes baking will produce a soufflé with a slightly runny centre – 40 minutes will result in it being firm all the way through. This could, however, vary slightly with your own particular oven, so it is best to take a quick look after about 25 minutes.

Cooked orange sauce

Metric	Imperial	USA	
1	1	1	small orange
15ml	1tbsp	1tbsp	olive oil
1	1	1	large onion, peeled and chopped
1	1	1	garlic clove, peeled and crushed
30ml	2tbsp	2tbsp	dry white wine
30ml	2tbsp	2tbsp	double [heavy] cream
10ml	2tsp	2tsp	sugar
			salt and freshly ground black pepper
25g	1oz	2tbsp	butter, cut into small pieces

Preparation time: 1¼ hours plus cooling

1 Boil the orange whole in water to cover for 1 hour. Drain and cool, then cut in half. Discard one half.

2 Heat the oil in a saucepan and cook the onion till transparent. Add the garlic and wine, cover and cook over a low heat for 5 minutes.

3 Place the orange half, onion and wine mixture, cream and sugar in a blender or food processor and blend until smooth. Pour into the saucepan, season with salt and pepper and reheat. Stir in the pieces of butter till melted, then serve hot.

Ratatouille niçoise

	Metric	Imperial	USA
olive oil	22.5ml	1½tbsp	1½tbsp
onions, peeled and chopped	2	2	2
garlic cloves, peeled and crushed	2	2	2
courgettes [zucchini] cut into 2.5cm/1 inch pieces	4	4	4
aubergines [eggplants], cut into 2.5cm/1 inch cubes	2	2	2
red or green peppers, cored, seeded and cut into 2.5cm/1 inch pieces	2	2	2
black olives	100-175g	4-6oz	1 cup
bay leaves	2	2	2
pinch of dried thyme, or 5ml/1tsp chopped fresh thyme, if available			
chopped fresh basil (if available)	15ml	1tbsp	1tbsp
tomato juice	600ml	1 pint	2½ cups
salt and freshly ground black pepper			
can tuna fish, drained and cubed	200-g	7-oz	7-oz
chopped parsley, to garnish			

1 Heat the oil in a saucepan and cook the onions until transparent. Add the garlic, courgettes, aubergines, peppers, olives, bay leaves, thyme, and basil (if used). Pour over the tomato juice and season with salt and pepper.
2 Bring to the boil, cover and simmer over a low heat for 30 minutes.
3 To serve, pour into a hot serving dish or on to 6 hot plates and top with tuna pieces and chopped parsley.

Preparation time: 50-60 minutes

Ricotta cheese and fresh fruit

	Metric	Imperial	USA
ricotta cheese	700g	1½lb	1½lb
plain·low-fat yogurt	45ml	3tbsp	3tbsp
a selection of seasonal fruit such as orange segments, strawberries, apple and peach slices, grapes, plums etc, prepared for eating easily			

1 Whip the cheese with the yogurt until creamy. Chill for at least 2 hours.
2 To serve, spoon some of the cheese mixture on to 6 large plates. Arrange the fruit around the plate and serve.

Preparation time: 20 minutes plus chilling

PUTTING ON THE STYLE

Right: top right, and then clockwise:
Cheese roulade with Waldorf filling; Strawberries in Champagne; Trifle; Salmon three ways; Mushroom-stuffed brioche ring; Turkey breast with confetti vegetable stuffing and Red and green salad; pp128-132.

PULLING OUT THE STOPS Party menu for 24 people
Mushroom-stuffed brioche ring
Salmon three ways
Cheese roulade with Waldorf filling
Turkey breast with confetti vegetable stuffing
Red and green salad
Trifle
Strawberries in Champagne

Mushroom-stuffed brioche ring

(Make 4)

Metric	Imperial	USA	
25g	1oz	2tbsp	butter
100g	4oz	1 cup	mushrooms, wiped and sliced
2	2	2	garlic cloves, peeled and crushed
			salt and freshly ground black pepper
350g	12oz	2⅓ cups	flour
2.5ml	½tsp	½tsp	salt
7.5ml	1½tsp	1½tsp	easy-blend dried yeast [active dry yeast]
5ml	1tsp	1tsp	sugar
3	3	3	eggs, beaten
75g	3oz	6tbsp	melted butter
30ml	2tbsp	2tbsp	hot water

Oven temperature: 230°C/
450°F/Gas Mark 8
Preparation time: 1 hour plus
rising

1 Heat the butter in a small saucepan, add the mushrooms and garlic and season with salt and pepper. Cover and cook over a low heat for 5 minutes, shaking the pan occasionally. Cool.

2 Mix the flour, salt, yeast and sugar in a large bowl, then mix in 2 of the eggs, the melted butter and the water. Work together to form a soft dough and knead on a floured surface for 10 minutes. (This process is easily done in a food processor.)

3 Roll out the dough into a strip about 30 × 15cm/12 × 6 inches. Spoon the mushroom mixture down the centre. Dampen the long edges and fold them over the filling. Lift the dough and place seam down in a ring mould, butting the two ends together. Cover and leave to rise in a warm place for about 2 hours or until doubled in size.

4 Brush the remaining beaten egg over the top of the dough. Bake in the oven for about 15 minutes or until cooked and golden brown.

NOTE As these are best served hot, they can be made a few hours in advance, removed from the moulds and reheated briefly before serving.

Salmon three ways (Make 3)

	Metric	Imperial	USA
smoked salmon, thinly sliced	225-275g	8-10oz	8-10oz
unflavoured gelatine	1 sachet	1 sachet	1 env.
white wine	60ml	4tbsp	1/4 cup
fresh salmon fillet, skinned	175g	6oz	6oz
salt and white pepper			
double [heavy] cream, whipped until stiff	300ml	1/2 pint	1 1/4 cups
salmon eggs [caviar]	25g	2tbsp	2tbsp
lemon juice	30ml	2tbsp	2tbsp

1 Line an oiled 600ml/1 pint [2 1/2-cup] loaf tin with oiled cling film [plastic wrap]. Carefully line this with the smoked salmon, leaving enough hanging over the edges to bring over and cover the filling completely.
2 Dissolve the gelatine in the white wine. Place in a blender or food processor with the fresh salmon and salt and pepper to taste and blend until smooth. Fold in the whipped cream.
3 Pour into the lined tin and level the top. Bring over the smoked salmon to cover the filling completely. Chill until set – at least 6 hours.
4 Turn out and slice. Arrange on 6 plates. Spoon on the salmon eggs, squeeze a little lemon juice over and serve immediately.
NOTE Red lumpfish roe makes a much cheaper and adequate substitute for the salmon eggs.

Preparation time: 30 minutes plus chilling

Cheese roulade with Waldorf filling (Make 3)

	Metric	Imperial	USA
grated Parmesan cheese			
fresh brown breadcrumbs	50g	2oz	1 cup
mature Cheddar cheese, grated	175g	6oz	1 1/2 cups
eggs, separated	4	4	4
double [heavy] cream	150ml	1/4 pint	2/3 cup
warm water	30ml	2tbsp	2tbsp
dry English mustard	2.5ml	1/2tsp	1/2tsp
salt and white pepper			
lettuce leaves			
The filling			
celery, finely chopped	100g	4oz	1 cup
apple, cored and finely chopped	100g	4oz	1 cup
walnuts, chopped	50g	2oz	1/2 cup
lemon juice	5ml	1tsp	1tsp
mayonnaise (see page 158)	60ml	4tbsp	1/4 cup

Oven temperature: 200°C/
400°F/Gas Mark 6
Preparation time: 45 minutes
plus cooling

1 Lightly oil a Swiss [jelly] roll tin, measuring about 33×23cm/13×9 inches. Line with oiled greaseproof [parchment] paper, snipping into the corners and allowing the paper to stick up about 2.5cm/1 inch above the sides of the tin. Sprinkle with a little Parmesan.

2 Mix the breadcrumbs, Cheddar cheese, egg yolks and cream together. Stir in the water and season with the mustard and salt and pepper to taste. Beat the egg whites until stiff and fold into the mixture. Pour into the lined tin and smooth with a knife.

3 Bake in the oven for 10-15 minutes or until firm.

4 Remove from the oven and cool for 5 minutes, then cover with a well rung out damp tea towel. Leave to cool completely – about 1 hour.

5 Meanwhile, make the filling by mixing together all the ingredients.

6 Sprinkle more Parmesan on a clean dry tea towel and turn out the cheese 'cake' on to this. Spread the filling evenly over the surface of the 'cake' and, with the help of the towel, roll up like a Swiss roll.

7 To serve, cut into slices and garnish with lettuce leaves.

Turkey breast with confetti vegetable stuffing

(Make 3)

Metric	Imperial	USA	
1	1	1	boneless turkey breast roast, about 700g/1½lb
1	1	1	spring onion [scallion], trimmed and chopped
50g	2oz	½ cup	carrot, scraped and cut into small dice
50g	2oz	½ cup	swede [rutabaga], peeled and cut into small dice
50g	2oz	½ cup	red pepper, cored, seeded and cut into small dice
25g	1oz	¼ cup	celery, cut into small dice
50g	2oz	½ cup	peas
350g	12oz	12oz	ricotta cheese
1	1	1	egg, beaten
10ml	2tsp	2tsp	green peppercorns
			salt

Preparation time: 45 minutes
plus cooling

1 With a very sharp knife, cut horizontally through the turkey breast, but not quite through. Open out like a book. Place on a dampened work surface and pound with a wet rolling pin to make the meat as large and thin as possible without breaking it. Trim away any really untidy bits and reserve these for another use.

2 Cook all the vegetables in boiling water for 5 minutes. Drain and dry very thoroughly.

3 Mix the ricotta well with the egg until very smooth. Mix in all the vegetables and the peppercorns and season with salt.

4 Pile this stuffing lengthways down the centre of the flattened turkey breast. Bring up the sides to cover the stuffing and make as neat a roll as possible. If necessary secure with wooden cocktail sticks or sew with thread.

5 Wrap the roll tightly in oiled foil. Steam for 45 minutes, and allow to cool.

6 To serve, slice thinly and arrange on a serving plate.

NOTE This quantity serves about 8 people.

Red and green salad

a selection of red salad ingredients as available, such as red cabbage, red onions, radicchio, tomatoes, red pepper, radishes, etc, prepared and chopped or sliced as liked

a selection of green salad ingredients as available, such as different lettuces, cresses, baby spinach leaves, chicory [Belgian endive], dandelion leaves, cucumber, green pepper, spring onions [scallions] etc., prepared and chopped or sliced as liked

vinaigrette dressing (see page 158)

Keep the red and green salads separate in 2 or more bowls and toss with the vinaigrette at the last minute.

NOTE The quantity of vinaigrette will depend on the quantity of salad made, but it is always better to make more dressing than is needed. Keep the surplus in a screw-top jar.

Preparation time: 20 minutes

Trifle

(Make 3)

Metric	Imperial	USA	
225g	8oz	4-6	trifle sponges [slices sponge or pound cake]
175g	6oz	½ cup	low-sugar raspberry jam
150ml	¼ pint	⅔ cup	dry or medium sherry
300ml	½ pint	1¼ cups	double [heavy] cream, whipped until stiff
			flaked [slivered] almonds

The custard

Metric	Imperial	USA	
900ml	1½ pints	3¾ cups	milk
3	3	3	egg yolks
22.5ml	1½tbsp	1½tbsp	sugar
22.5ml	1½tbsp	1½tbsp	cornflour [cornstarch]
3.75ml	¾tsp	¾tsp	vanilla essence [extract]

Preparation time: 25-30 minutes plus chilling

1 Slice each sponge [cake slice] in half across and spread thickly with jam. Arrange, jam side up, in the bottom of a glass bowl and pour over the sherry.

2 To make the custard, bring the milk to boiling point in a saucepan. While this is heating, whisk the egg yolks with the sugar, cornflour and vanilla essence until pale. When the milk is almost boiling, pour it in a steady stream on to the egg mixture, whisking all the time. Strain through a sieve back into the saucepan and cook over the lowest possible heat until thickened. This custard will not go lumpy if stirred all the time it is cooking. Allow to cool a little.

3 Pour the cooled custard over the sherry-soaked sponges, prodding the sponges a little with a fork to ensure the custard seeps right down through every space to the bottom of the bowl. Chill to set.

4 Cover with whipped cream and garnish with flaked almonds.

Strawberries in Champagne

Metric	Imperial	USA	
1.8kg	4lb	4lb	strawberries, hulled and sliced if larger than bite-size
2	2	2	bottles Champagne, chilled

Preparation time: 20 minutes plus chilling

1 Fill 24 champagne flutes or other suitable glasses with the whole or sliced strawberries and chill.

2 Just before serving fill up the glasses with cold Champagne. Provide long-handled spoons for the strawberries. The Champagne can be drunk from the glass at the end.

Truffled mushrooms in the half shell
Assiette des fruits de terre
Home-made cream cheese balls
in olive oil with fresh herbs
Frozen strawberry and pink Champagne soufflé

Truffled mushrooms in the half shell

	Metric	Imperial	USA
quantity shortcrust [basic pie] pastry (see page 156)	1	1	1
butter	75g	3oz	6tbsp
spring onions [scallions], trimmed and chopped	2	2	2
dried Chinese or Italian mushrooms, soaked for 30 minutes in warm water, drained, hard stems discarded and sliced	4	4	4
button mushrooms, wiped and sliced	275g	10oz	2½ cups
black truffle (as much as you can afford), chopped or sliced			
salt and freshly ground black pepper			
chopped parsley	30ml	2tbsp	2tbsp
radicchio or other salad leaves in season			

1 Roll out the pastry thinly, then use to cover the backs of 6 well-scrubbed oiled and floured scallop shells. Arrange on a baking sheet and bake in the oven for 10-15 minutes or until pale golden. Cool and carefully remove from the shells. Place hollow side up on a baking sheet ready to reheat just before serving.

2 Melt the butter in a saucepan and cook the onions for 2 minutes. Add all the mushrooms and most of the truffle (keeping a little back for garnish). Season with salt and pepper. Cover and cook over a low heat for 10 minutes, shaking the pan occasionally.

3 Just before serving, reheat the pastry shells.

4 Remove the pastry shells from the oven and divide the hot mushroom mixture between them. Sprinkle with a little parsley and the reserved truffle.

5 Arrange a little salad on each plate. Place a shell in the centre of this and serve immediately.

NOTE Though not quite as luxurious, this recipe is quite delicious if the truffle is omitted.

Oven temperature: 220°C/425°F/Gas Mark 7
Preparation time: 1 hour plus cooling

Left: Truffled mushrooms in the half shell; p133.
Above: Assiette des fruits de terre; p136.
Right: Home-made cream cheese balls in olive oil with fresh herbs; p137.

Assiette des fruits de terre

Metric	Imperial	USA	
6	6	6	globe artichokes
300ml	½ pint	1¼ cups	mayonnaise (see page 158)
3	3	3	garlic cloves, peeled and crushed
45ml	3tbsp	3tbsp	double [heavy] cream
1	1	1	head endive or frisée [chicory], broken into pieces
6	6	6	large, uncooked spears fresh asparagus (or 12 small spears)
1	1	1	fennel bulb, sliced
6	6	6	celery stalks, cut into 5cm/2 inch sticks
900g	2lb	2lb	new potatoes, cooked in skins and cooled
1	1	1	bunch radishes, leaves left on
225g	8oz	8oz	cherry tomatoes
1	1	1	head chicory (Belgian endive), leaves separated

Preparation time: 1¼-1½ hours plus cooling .

1 Trim the stalks of the artichokes level with the base and cook in boiling salted water for about 45 minutes or until a leaf near the base can be pulled away easily. Drain and cool, upside-down.

2 Pull out the centre leaves from each artichoke and carefully remove the prickly 'chokes'.

3 Place the artichokes down the centre of a very long serving platter (a tray will do).

4 Mix the mayonnaise with the garlic and cream and pour this into the cavities of the artichokes. Cover the rest of the tray with the pieces of endive or frisée. Arrange all the other vegetables attractively around the artichokes.

5 To serve, place the 'assiette' in the centre of the table. Each guest helps himself or herself, dipping the various vegetables into the garlic mayonnaise in the artichoke, then dipping in the edible leaf tips of the artichoke and finally eating the artichoke base.

NOTE These ingredients are merely a guide line. Vary the vegetables as available.

Home-made cream cheese balls in olive oil with fresh herbs

	Metric	Imperial	USA
creamy milk, warmed to blood heat	1.8 litres	3 pints	7½ cups
lemon juice, strained	120ml	4fl oz	½ cup
salt and white pepper			
extra virgin olive oil	120ml	4fl oz	½ cup
chopped fresh green herbs, as varied as possible			

1 Put the milk in a bowl and stir in the lemon juice. Leave in a warm place for 30 minutes for the curds to form. Line a colander with a large square of muslin or cheesecloth and pour in the milk mixture. Discard the liquid whey that drains off. Bring up the four corners of the cloth and hang up to drain in a cool place for about 2 hours.

2 Tip the drained cheese into a bowl and mash well with a fork. Season with salt and pepper. Form into 24 little balls in the hands and place these in a layer in a shallow dish.

3 Sprinkle over the oil and herbs and leave at room temperature for 1-2 hours, occasionally 'basting' the cheese balls with the oil.

4 To serve, place 4 cheese balls on each plate. Spoon over the oil and sprinkle with more fresh herbs. Serve with good bread.

NOTE Sage and rosemary should not be included as they are unpleasantly strong in taste and have a bad texture for eating raw.

Preparation time: 1 hour plus draining and marinating

Frozen strawberry and pink Champagne soufflé

	Metric	Imperial	USA
strawberries	225g	8oz	8oz
double [heavy] cream, whipped till thick	300ml	½ pint	1¼ cups
brandy	45ml	3tbsp	3tbsp
pink Champagne (or white wine)	75ml	5tbsp	5tbsp
lemon juice	30ml	2tbsp	2tbsp
red or pink food colouring			
eggs, separated	4	4	4
caster [superfine] sugar	75g	3oz	½ cup

1 Tie a strip of greaseproof [wax] paper around the outside of a 1.2 litre/2 pint [5-cup] soufflé dish to come 7.5cm/3 inches above the rim of the dish.

2 Roughly chop the strawberries, reserving a few to halve and use as decoration. Set aside.

3 Place the cream, brandy, Champagne, lemon juice and a few drops of colouring in a bowl and whisk until quite stiff.

Preparation time: 30 minutes plus freezing

4 Beat the egg yolks with the sugar until pale and creamy, then fold into the cream mixture. Beat the egg whites until stiff and fold in. Finally, carefully fold in the chopped strawberries.

5 Pour into the prepared soufflé dish and freeze until firm.

6 Carefully remove the paper band and decorate the top of the soufflé with the reserved strawberry halves. Remove from the freezer to the refrigerator 20 minutes before required to soften a little.

NOTE Use pink Champagne if you want to be authentic, but still add a hint of food colour to make the finished soufflé pink.

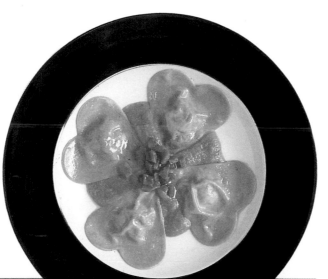

Left: top Mushroom
symphony; **below:**
Prelude in cheese; p140.

Above: Romantic
interlude; p141.
Left: Theme in
chocolate with three
variations; p142.

Prelude in cheese
Mushroom symphony
Romantic interlude
Theme in chocolate with three variations

Prelude in cheese

Metric	Imperial	USA	
450g	1lb	1lb	puff pastry, thawed if frozen
450g	1lb	1lb	goat's cheese, cut into 6 round slices
1	1	1	egg yolk, beaten
			fresh herbs in season (eg chervil and chives)
			redcurrant jelly

Oven temperature: 220°C/
425°F/Gas Mark 7
Preparation time: 45 minutes

1 Roll out the pastry thinly and cut out 12 rounds just a little larger than the slices of cheese.
2 Place the cheese in the centre of 6 of the pastry rounds. Dampen the edges of the pastry with water and place the remaining pastry rounds on top. Seal the edges by pressing lightly with the fingers. Flute the edges if liked and score a pattern on the top with the point of a knife. Brush with the egg yolk and make a small incision in the centre of each little 'pie'.
3 Place on a dampened baking sheet and bake in the oven for about 15 minutes or until puffed and golden.
4 To serve, place each little pie on a hot plate and garnish with herbs and a spoonful of redcurrant jelly.

Mushroom symphony

Metric	Imperial	USA	
			an assortment of seasonal salad leaves, as varied and interesting as possible
50g	2oz	4tbsp	butter
2	2	2	spring onions [scallions], trimmed and chopped
2	2	2	garlic cloves, peeled and crushed
100g	4oz	1 cup	button mushrooms, wiped and sliced
225g	8oz	8oz	canned Chinese straw mushrooms, drained
120ml	4floz	½ cup	single [light] cream
			salt and freshly ground black pepper
15ml	1tbsp	1tbsp	chopped parsley

Preparation time: 15 minutes

1 Tear the salad leaves into small pieces and arrange in a little 'nest' in the centre of 6 large plates.
2 Melt the butter in a frying pan over a medium heat and cook the onions

for 2 minutes, stirring. Add the garlic and mushrooms and continue to cook, stirring, for a further 2 minutes. Add the cream, salt and pepper to taste and parsley. Allow to bubble for 2 minutes.

3 To serve, pour some of the mushrooms and cream mixture into the middle of each salad 'nest' and serve immediately.

Romantic interlude

	Metric	Imperial	USA
flour	350g	12oz	2⅓ cups
eggs	3	3	3
concentrated tomato purée [paste]	45ml	3tbsp	3tbsp
salt	5ml	1tsp	1tsp
dried oregano	2.5ml	½tsp	½tsp
water (if needed)	15ml	1tbsp	1tbsp
cream cheese	75g	3oz	3oz
cooked salmon fillet, flaked	75g	3oz	3oz
spring onion [scallion], trimmed and finely chopped	1	1	1
salt and freshly ground black pepper			
quantity fresh tomato sauce (see page 41)	1	1	1
tomato, skinned, seeded and diced	1	1	1

1 Make a stiff dough with the flour, eggs, tomato purée, salt and dried oregano, adding the water only if the dough is too dry to handle. Knead 10 minutes. (This process can be very easily and quickly done in a food processor.)

2 Divide the dough in half and roll out each piece as thinly as possible. Hang the dough over a clean broom handle, supported between two chairs, and leave for 45 minutes to dry a little.

3 Meanwhile, make the stuffing. Mix the cream cheese with the salmon and onion and season with salt and pepper.

4 Lay 1 sheet of dough on a work surface. Make 24 little piles of filling on the dough, spacing them out as well as possible and using all the filling. Brush all around each pile of filling with water and lay the second sheet of dough on top.

5 Press all around each lump of filling to seal the two layers of dough together. Now cut out heart shapes with a metal cutter so that the filling is in the centre of each. Discard the rest of the dough.

6 Cook the hearts in a large pan of boiling salted water for 3 minutes. Meanwhile, reheat the tomato sauce.

7 To serve, divide the sauce between 6 hot plates and place 4 pasta hearts on top. Garnish with the raw diced tomato and serve immediately.

Preparation time: 50 minutes plus drying

Theme in chocolate with three variations

Metric	Imperial	USA	
90ml	6tbsp	6tbsp	single [light] cream
1 sachet	1 sachet	1 env.	unflavoured gelatine
75g	3oz	3oz	white chocolate, grated
300ml	½ pint	1 cup	double [heavy] cream, whipped until stiff
75g	3oz	3oz	milk chocolate, grated

			The sauce
150g	5oz	¾ cup	sugar
175ml	6floz	¾ cup	water
			grated rind of 1 small orange
100g	4oz	4oz	plain [semisweet] chocolate, broken into small pieces

Preparation time: 45 minutes
plus cooling and chilling

1 In a double boiler or a bowl placed over a pan of boiling water, heat half the cream with half the gelatine until dissolved. Add the white chocolate and stir well. Leave to cool slightly, then fold in half of the cream.

2 Pour this mixture into a 600ml/1 pint [2½-cup capacity] loaf tin or other suitable mould. Chill until beginning to set.

3 Repeat step 1 with the milk chocolate. Pour this over the white chocolate layer in the tin and chill for at least 6 hours or until set.

4 To make the sauce, put the sugar, water and orange rind in a saucepan and bring to the boil, stirring to dissolve the sugar. Boil over medium heat for 5 minutes. Add the chocolate and stir until melted. Cool.

5 To serve, dip the mould briefly in hot water, then turn out the mousse on to a flat work surface. Cut into 6 equal slices. Arrange these in the centre of the plates and surround with the sauce.

Right: top: Leek-stuffed pears with blue cheese sauce; **left:** Calvados and pheasant casserole en croûte and Tomato salad with tarragon vinegar; **right:** Fruit and nut port wine jelly; pp144-146.

Leek-stuffed pears with blue cheese sauce
Calvados and pheasant casserole en croûte
Tomato salad with tarragon vinegar
Fruit and nut port wine jelly

Leek-stuffed pears with blue cheese sauce

Metric	Imperial	USA	
15ml	1tbsp	1tbsp	olive oil
175g	6oz	6oz	leeks, washed and chopped
1	1	1	garlic clove, peeled and crushed
5ml	1tsp	1tsp	ground cumin
5ml	1tsp	1tsp	ground coriander
			salt and freshly ground black pepper
6	6	6	hard pears
600ml	1 pint	2½ cups	chicken or vegetable stock (see page 156)
1	1	1	quantity gorgonzola sauce (see page 12)

Preparation time: 1½ hours

1 Heat the oil in a small saucepan and cook the leeks with the garlic, cumin and coriander over a low heat for about 10 minutes, stirring occasionally. The leeks should be soft. Season with salt and pepper.

2 Meanwhile, peel the pears and with an apple corer remove a plug right through the centre.

3 Stuff the cavities in the pears with the leek mixture. Arrange the pears upright in a pan which will just accommodate them snugly in one layer. Pour over the stock but do not let it cover the pears.

4 Bring to the boil and turn down the heat so that the water is barely moving. Cover the pan tightly and cook for about 1 hour or until the pears are quite soft.

5 Gently lift the pears from the pan, being careful not to disturb the stuffing. Discard the pan liquids (or add to soups or sauces). Stand each pear, upright, on a heated plate and pour over some hot gorgonzola sauce.

Calvados and pheasant casserole en croûte

	Metric	Imperial	USA
large pheasant	1	1	1
small onion, peeled and quartered	1	1	1
bay leaf	1	1	1
strip of finely pared orange rind	7.5-cm	3-inch	3-inch
chopped fresh sage, or half that amount if using dried	2.5ml	½tsp	½tsp
butter	25g	1oz	2tbsp
small onion, peeled and chopped	1	1	1
button mushrooms, wiped and sliced	100g	4oz	1 cup
Calvados [or applejack] or brandy	120ml	4floz	½ cup
lemon juice	30ml	2tbsp	2tbsp
chopped parsley	30ml	2tbsp	2tbsp
salt and freshly ground black pepper			
quantity shortcrust [basic pie] pastry (see page 156)	1	1	1
crisp apples, peeled, cored and cut into small cubes	2	2	2
puff pastry, thawed if frozen	225g	8oz	8oz
egg yolk, mixed with a little milk	1	1	1

1 Remove all the meat from the pheasant, discarding all skin. Cut into bite-sized pieces. Set aside.

2 Place the pheasant carcass, quartered onion, bay leaf, orange rind and sage in a large saucepan. Cover with cold water and bring to the boil, skimming off any scum which rises to the surface. Cover and simmer over a low heat for 2 hours. Strain, discard the debris and chill the stock until the fat solidifies on the top – about 6 hours.

3 Remove the fat from the stock and discard. Pour the stock into a large saucepan and boil to reduce to 600ml/1 pint [2½ cups] over a high heat.

4 Meanwhile, melt the butter in a saucepan and cook the chopped onion over a medium heat until transparent. Add the mushrooms and cook for 2 minutes, stirring occasionally. Add the pieces of pheasant meat and continue to cook for about 5 minutes, stirring, or until the meat is sealed all over.

5 Pour over the Calvados, heat briefly and light with a match (stand well back). When the flames have died down, add the reduced stock to the pan with the lemon juice and parsley. Season with salt and pepper to taste. Cover and simmer over a low heat for 1 hour. Pour the contents of the pan into a bowl and allow to cool.

6 Roll out the shortcrust [pie] pastry, but not too thinly, and use to line 6 loose-bottomed medium patty tins [tartlet pans].

7 Add the apple to the cooked pheasant mixture and check the

Oven temperature: 190°C/
375°F/Gas Mark 5
Preparation time: 4½ hours
plus chilling

seasoning. Spoon into the lined tins and pour over only a little of the gravy.

8 Roll out the puff pastry and cut out 6 rounds just big enough to cover each little pie. Dampen the edges of the pastry in the tins with a little egg yolk and milk mixture and press on the puff pastry lids. Make a little slit in the top of each pie and brush with the egg and milk to glaze.

9 Bake in the oven for about 30 minutes or until the pastry is golden and crisp.

10 Carefully remove the pies from the tins, place on hot plates and serve with tomato salad with tarragon vinegar (see following recipe) and the remaining gravy, reheated and handed separately in a sauceboat.

Tomato salad with tarragon vinegar

Metric	Imperial	USA	
900g	2lb	2lb	ripe tomatoes, thinly sliced
1	1	1	quantity vinaigrette dressing (see page 158), made with tarragon vinegar
			fresh tarragon leaves or chopped chives

Preparation time: 10 minutes plus marinating

1 Place the tomato slices in a bowl and pour over the dressing. Leave at room temperature for at least 1 hour for the flavours to develop.

2 Just before serving, sprinkle with tarragon leaves or chopped chives.

Fruit and nut port wine jelly

Metric	Imperial	USA	
225g	8oz	8oz	mixed dried fruit
350ml	12floz	1½ cups	port
120ml	4floz	½ cup	water
1 sachet	1 sachet	1 env.	unflavoured gelatine
50g	2oz	½ cup	flaked [slivered] almonds

Preparation time: 15 minutes plus soaking and chilling

1 Put the dried fruit in a bowl and pour over the port. Cover closely and leave to soak for 4-6 hours.

2 Heat the water in a small pan and dissolve the gelatine over a low heat.

3 Stir the gelatine mixture into the port and fruit mixture. Add the almonds.

4 Pour into 6 small glasses or moulds. If you wish to turn the jellies out, chill till set – at least 6 hours.

Above: Warm duck breast salad with raspberries; p148.

Warm duck breast salad with raspberries
Smoked salmon and garlic parcels
Feuilleté of root vegetable with its purée
Two melon vinaigrete
Stilton soufflés

Warm duck breast salad with raspberries

Metric	Imperial	USA	
2 450-g	2 1-lb	2 1-lb	boneless duck breasts with skin [duck breast halves]
50g	2oz	4tbsp	butter
½	½	½	small onion, peeled and chopped
1	1	1	garlic clove, peeled and crushed
60ml	4tbsp	¼ cup	raspberry vinegar
45ml	3tbsp	3tbsp	walnut oil
			salt and freshly ground black pepper
			a selection of seasonal salad greens, as available
175g	6oz	6oz	raspberries, thawed if frozen

Preparation time: 45 minutes

1 Prick the skin of the duck breasts all over and rub with salt. Place skin side down in a grill [broiler] pan without the rack. Cook under a low to medium grill [broiler] for 10 minutes, then turn over so the skin side is up and cook for a further 15 minutes. If the skin is not crispy near the end, turn up the heat for the last few minutes.

2 Meanwhile, melt the butter in a frying pan and cook the onion until transparent. Add the garlic and vinegar, turn up the heat and allow to bubble furiously until the liquid is reduced by half. (This process makes quite a pungent smell in the kitchen.) Turn the heat down to low and add the walnut oil. Season with salt and pepper and heat until just bubbling. When the duck breasts are cooked, add 15ml/1tbsp of the duck fat to the hot dressing in the pan.

3 Slice the duck breast diagonally across as thinly as possible.

4 Make a little 'nest' of salad greens in the middle of 6 large plates. Arrange the hot duck slices on the salad, scatter on the raspberries and drizzle over the hot dressing. Serve at once.

NOTE Duck breasts are available in large supermarkets, or cut the breasts off a duck and reserve the rest of the bird for a casserole or pâté.

Smoked salmon and garlic parcels

	Metric	Imperial	USA
garlic cloves, peeled and crushed	2	2	2
butter, softened	40g	1½oz	3tbsp
smoked salmon, thinly sliced	175g	6oz	6oz
fresh white breadcrumbs	150g	5oz	2½ cups
grated lemon rind	2.5ml	½tsp	½tsp
lemon juice	15ml	1tbsp	1tbsp
eggs, beaten	2	2	2
white pepper			
oil for deep frying			

1 Beat the garlic into the softened butter and chill till hard.

2 Cut 6 rectangles from the smoked salmon, each measuring 7.5×5cm/ 3×2 inches. Set aside.

3 Place the remaining salmon in a blender or food processor with the breadcrumbs, lemon rind and juice, eggs and a little pepper and process until fairly smooth. You should have a moist mixture, but if it is too sloppy to handle, add a few more breadcrumbs.

4 Cut 6 little sticks, each 5cm/2 inches long, from the chilled garlic butter. Lay one on the end of each rectangle of smoked salmon and roll up so the butter is completely enclosed.

5 Spoon one sixth of the breadcrumb mixture into the palm of one hand and pat it out flat with the other hand. Place a salmon/butter roll in the middle and bring the crumb mixture round to encase it completely. Make sure there are no holes (this is a little messy, but not difficult). Arrange on a plate and chill for 1 hour or more.

6 Deep fry in hot oil for 3-4 minutes, turning once, or until deep golden and crispy on the outside. Drain on paper towels and serve hot, with Feuillette of root vegetable and Two melon vinaigrette as a side dish (see following recipes).

NOTE If these are made carefully, the garlic butter will have remained in its little pocket inside, but melted to escape in a delicious pool when cut open.

Preparation time: about 30 minutes plus chilling

Feuilleté of root vegetable with its purée

Metric	Imperial	USA	
1	1	1	swede [rutabaga], peeled
4	4	4	large carrots, scraped
4	4	4	large parsnips, peeled
225g	8oz	8oz	puff pastry, thawed if frozen
1	1	1	egg yolk, beaten with a little milk
50g	2oz	4tbsp	butter
			salt and white pepper
			grated nutmeg

Oven temperature: 220°C/
425°F/Gas Mark 7
Preparation time: 45 minutes

1 With an apple corer, cut little barrel shapes from the vegetables, about 6.5cm/2½ inches long. There should be 2 barrels of each vegetable per person. Cook the barrels in boiling water until tender.

2 Cut the rest of the vegetables (the 'debris') into even-sized pieces and cook in another saucepan of boiling salted water. When tender, drain.

3 Meanwhile, roll out the pastry thinly and cut out 6 diamond shapes, each side about 5cm/2 inch long. Score with a knife and brush with egg yolk glaze. Place on a dampened baking sheet and bake in the oven for about 15 minutes or until well risen and golden brown. Split each pastry diamond in half so that you have bases and lids.

4 Purée the cooked vegetable 'debris' with the butter and season with salt, pepper and nutmeg. Drain the vegetable barrels.

5 To serve, place a pastry base on each plate, spoon over some of the purée, allowing it to spill out a little, and replace the pastry lids. Arrange the vegetable barrels attractively in front of the filled pastry.

NOTE If you do not have the time or energy to make the barrels, cut sticks 1×1×6.5cm/½×½×2½ inches instead.

Two melon vinaigrette

	Metric	Imperial	USA
sweet ripe melon, such as honeydew, ogen, charentais or canteloupe	575-700g	1 1/4-1 1/2lb	1 1/4-1 1/2lb
ripe watermelon	575-700g	1 1/4-1 1/2lb	1 1/4-1 1/2lb
quantity vinaigrette dressing, including garlic (see page 158)	1	1	1

1 Remove the seeds from the sweet melon and either cut into balls with a melon baller, or peel and cut into cubes.

2 Cut the watermelon into balls or cubes, and carefully remove the seeds from the pieces.

3 Place both kinds of melon in a bowl and pour over the dressing. Toss to coat and chill for at least 1 hour.

4 Serve in small bowls or on small plates.

NOTE There is always wastage if you use a melon baller; therefore, it would be necessary to buy 700g/1 1/2lb of each kind of melon. If you cut the melon into cubes, however, 575g/1 1/4lb would be sufficient.

Preparation time: 20 minutes plus chilling

Stilton soufflés

	Metric	Imperial	USA
butter	25g	1oz	2tbsp
flour	15g	1/2oz	1 1/2tbsp
milk	150ml	1/4 pint	2/3 cup
eggs, separated	3	3	3
Stilton cheese, grated	100g	4oz	1 cup
salt and freshly ground black pepper			

1 Melt the butter in a saucepan over a medium heat, add the flour and cook, stirring, for 2 minutes. Add the milk and bring to the boil, stirring constantly to ensure that no lumps form. Turn down the heat to low and simmer very gently for 2 minutes, still stirring. Allow to cool for 5 minutes.

2 Beat in the egg yolks and cheese with salt and pepper to taste. Beat the egg whites until stiff and fold into the mixture.

3 Pour immediately into 6 well-buttered individual soufflé dishes. Bake in the oven for 15 minutes or until well risen and golden brown. Serve immediately.

NOTE Everything can be prepared in advance except the egg whites. So 15 minutes before you are ready to eat the soufflés, beat the whites, fold them in and bake the soufflés.

Oven temperature: 190°C/375°F/Gas Mark 5.
Preparation time: about 30 minutes

Artichoke and truffle salad
Steamed scallops with lime marmalade sauce
Two vegetable timbales
Grapes on gingered shortcake

Artichoke and truffle salad

Metric	Imperial	USA	
			black truffle, sliced (as much as possible)
1	1	1	quantity vinaigrette dressing without garlic (see page 158)
			an assortment of salad leaves, as varied and interesting as possible
225g	8oz	8oz	artichoke bottoms, drained if canned, cut into 5mm/ ¼ inch slices

Preparation time: 15 minutes plus marinating

1 Place the truffle slices (if used) in a bowl. Pour over the dressing, cover closely and leave at room temperature for at least 6 hours for flavours to develop.

2 Tear the leaves into small pieces and arrange in a little 'nest' in the centre of 6 large plates.

3 Arrange the artichoke slices on top of the 'nests'. Drizzle over the dressing, making sure that everyone gets their fair share of truffle slices.
NOTE Though this salad is naturally not nearly so glamorous without the truffle, it is nevertheless delicious.

Steamed scallops with lime marmalade sauce

Metric	Imperial	USA	
15ml	1 tbsp	1 tbsp	olive oil
½	½	½	small onion, peeled and chopped
1	1	1	garlic clove, peeled and crushed
2.5-cm	1-inch	1-inch	cube fresh ginger, peeled and finely chopped
150ml	¼ pint	⅔ cup	white wine
150ml	¼ pint	⅔ cup	chicken or vegetable stock (see page 156)
30ml	2 tbsp	2 tbsp	lime marmalade (or more to taste)
			salt and white pepper
5ml	1 tsp	1 tsp	arrowroot
			juice of 1 lemon
18	18	18	scallops, removed from shell (thawed if frozen)
15ml	1 tbsp	1 tbsp	finely chopped parsley

1 Heat the oil in a frying pan and cook the onion over a medium heat until transparent. Add the garlic, ginger and wine. Turn up the heat and bubble furiously until the wine is reduced by half. Add the stock and marmalade and season with salt and pepper. Cook over a medium heat, stirring, for 2-3 minutes.

2 Dissolve the arrowroot in half of the lemon juice and stir into the sauce. Continue to cook for 2 minutes until the sauce thickens slightly.

3 Meanwhile, arrange the scallops in one layer on a lightly oiled plate arranged on a steamer. Sprinkle over the parsley, remaining lemon juice and salt and pepper to taste. Steam for 5 minutes.

4 To serve, arrange 3 scallops on one side of each hot plate and spoon over the hot sauce. Serve with two vegetable timbales (see following recipe).

Preparation time: 25-30 minutes

Two vegetable timbales

	Metric	Imperial	USA
puréed cooked broad [or lima] beans	250ml	8fl oz	1 cup
puréed cooked carrots	250ml	8fl oz	1 cup
double [heavy] cream	300ml	½ pint	1¼ cups
eggs, beaten	3	3	3
salt and white pepper			

1 Place the bean purée in a bowl and the carrot purée in another bowl. Add half the cream and eggs to each bowl and season to taste with salt and pepper. Mix well.

2 Butter 6 individual ramekins or moulds and place a circle of buttered greaseproof [parchment] paper in the bottom of each. Pour in the two different vegetable mixtures in separate layers. (When cooked they will not be in exactly level stripes, but the colours should be distinctly separate.) Cover each pot with a circle of buttered foil.

3 Bake in a bain-marie in the oven for 30-40 minutes or until set.

NOTE It is difficult to give exact quantities of vegetable to supply 250ml/8fl oz [1 cup] of purée, but 425g/14oz should be enough. Any surplus can be reheated as a vegetable or made into a soup or sauce. It is very important that the purées should be as dry as possible.

Oven temperature: 170°C/ 325°F/Gas Mark 3
Preparation time: 1-1¼ hours

Grapes on gingered shortcake

	Metric	Imperial	USA
flour	175g	6oz	1 1/4 cups
caster [superfine] sugar	50g	2oz	1/3 cup
pinch of salt			
butter	100g	4oz	8tbsp
pieces stem ginger preserved in syrup, chopped	3	3	3
plain thick Greek-style yogurt	45ml	3tbsp	3tbsp
green grapes, halved and seeded (or more)	21	21	21

1 Place the flour, sugar and salt in a bowl and rub in the butter. Add the pieces of ginger just as the dough is forming.

2 Divide the dough into 6 equal portions and form into balls. Roll these out on a work surface sprinkled with caster [superfine] sugar until they form large rounds about 5mm/1/4 inch thick. Prick all over with a fork and arrange on a buttered baking sheet. Bake in the oven for 40-50 minutes or until crisp and golden.

3 Remove carefully to a wire cake rack and cool.

4 To serve, place a shortcake in the centre of each plate. Smooth 7.5ml/1/2tbsp of yogurt in the centre and surround this with a circle of grape halves.

NOTE Step 1 can be done in a food processor.

Oven temperature: 150°C/ 300°F/Gas Mark 2
Preparation time: 1 1/4 hours plus cooling

Left: top: Steamed scallops with lime marmalade sauce and Two vegetable timbale; **centre:** Grapes on gingered shortcake; **below:** Artichoke and truffle salad; pp152-155.

Shortcrust [basic pie] pastry (Makes 450g/1lb)

Metric	Imperial	USA	
225g	8oz	1⅔ cups	flour
3.75ml	¾tsp	¾tsp	salt
100g	4oz	8tbsp	cold butter, cut into small pieces
1	1	1	egg yolk, lightly beaten
45ml	3tbsp	3tbsp	cold water

Preparation time: 5-10 minutes plus chilling

1 Place the flour and salt in a mixing bowl and rub in the butter until the mixture resembles fine breadcrumbs.
2 Mix in the egg yolk and water – adding more if necessary – and, working quickly, bring together the mixture until it forms a smooth dough.
3 Wrap and chill for 30 minutes before rolling out.
NOTE This can be made in a food processor.

Sweet pastry (Makes 450g/1lb)

Metric	Imperial	USA	
225g	8oz	1⅔ cups	flour
			pinch of salt
30ml	2tbsp	2tbsp	caster [superfine] sugar
100g	4oz	8tbsp	cold unsalted butter, cut into small pieces
1	1	1	egg yolk, lightly beaten
30ml	2tbsp	2tbsp	cold water

Preparation time: 5-10 minutes plus chilling

1 Place the flour, salt and sugar in a mixing bowl and rub in the butter until the mixture resembles fine breadcrumbs.
2 Mix in the egg yolk and water – adding more if necessary – and, working quickly, bring together the mixture until it forms a smooth dough.
3 Wrap and chill for 30 minutes before rolling out.
NOTE This can be made in a food processor.

Chicken stock (Makes 1.8 litres/3 pints [2 quarts])

Metric	Imperial	USA	
1 2.25-kg	1 5-lb	1 5-lb	large boiling chicken with giblets, cut into 8 pieces
1	1	1	onion, washed but with the skin left on, quartered
2	2	2	garlic cloves, peeled but left whole
1	1	1	carrot, scrubbed and roughly chopped
1	1	1	celery stalk, chopped (optional)
5-cm	2-inch	2-inch	strip finely pared lemon rind
10ml	2tsp	2tsp	salt
			freshly ground pepper (white, if available, is preferable to black as it does not leave dark specks in the finished stock)
1.8 litres	3 pints	2 quarts	cold water

1 Place all the ingredients in a very large saucepan and slowly bring to the boil, skimming off any scum as it rises to the surface. Cover the pan tightly and cook over a gentle heat for 2 hours. Alternatively, cook in a slow cooker on low for 8 hours or overnight.

Preparation time: 2½ hours plus cooling and chilling

2 Remove the chicken. Take the meat from the bones and discard all the skin. Reserve the meat for another use.

3 Strain the stock and discard the solids.

4 Chill the stock for at least 4 hours after it has cooled, preferably overnight, then remove the fat which will have solidified on the surface. The stock is now ready for use.

NOTE Other vegetables and herbs can be added to this recipe, but this version uses only vegetables available all year round. Leaving on the onion skins adds a rich golden colour to the stock.

Vegetable stock

(Makes 1.8 litres/3 pints [2 quarts])

	Metric	Imperial	USA
mushrooms, wiped and sliced	100g	4oz	1 cup
onions, washed but skins left on, quartered	450g	1lb	1lb
carrots, scrubbed and roughly chopped	225g	8oz	8oz
swede [rutabaga] or turnip, peeled and roughly chopped	225g	8oz	8oz
celery stalks, roughly chopped	2	2	2
green or red pepper, cored, seeded and roughly chopped	½	½	½
garlic cloves, peeled but left whole	3	3	3
strip finely pared lemon rind	5-cm	2-inch	2-inch
large bunch of parsley	1	1	1
bay leaf	1	1	1
salt	5ml	1tsp	1tsp
sugar	5ml	1tsp	1tsp
freshly ground pepper (white if available is preferable to black as it does not leave dark specks in the finished stock)			
cold water	1.8 litres	3 pints	2 quarts
dash of soy sauce			

1 Place all the ingredients in a very large saucepan. Bring to the boil, then cover the pan tightly and simmer gently for 1½ hours.

Preparation time: 2 hours

2 Strain the stock and discard the solids. The stock is now ready for use. The ingredients for this stock only include basic vegetables and herbs which are easily available all year, but the addition of more fresh produce as available will produce a more interesting stock.

Vinaigrette dressing (Makes 60ml/4tbsp)

Metric	Imperial	USA	
15ml	1tbsp	1tbsp	lemon juice
45ml	3tbsp	3tbsp	olive oil, or half olive oil and half vegetable oil
2.5ml	½tsp	½tsp	sugar
1	1	1	garlic clove, peeled and crushed (optional)
1.25ml	¼tsp	¼tsp	dry English mustard
2.5ml	½tsp	½tsp	salt
1.25ml	¼tsp	¼tsp	freshly ground black pepper

Preparation time: 5 minutes

1 Place all the ingredients in a screw-topped jar and shake till amalgamated, or place in a bowl and whisk. Leave at least 1 hour for flavours to develop before using.

NOTE This recipe can easily be varied to make a whole range of exciting dressings, by trying different oils, such as nut oils, and flavoured vinegars, eg raspberry or tarragon, or adding chopped fresh herbs.

Mayonnaise (Makes 250ml/8floz [1 cup])

Metric	Imperial	USA	
2	2	2	eggs, at room temperature
10ml	2tsp	2tsp	salt
5ml	1tsp	1tsp	dry English mustard
150ml	¼ pint	⅔ cup	best olive oil
150ml	¼ pint	⅔ cup	tasteless vegetable oil
			juice of ½ lemon
			freshly ground pepper (white if available is preferable to black as it does not leave dark specks)

Preparation time: 5 minutes

1 Place the eggs, salt and mustard in a blender or food processor and blend until smooth.

2 With the motor running, add the oils in a very thin steady trickle. You can pour them in a little quicker as the mayonnaise begins to thicken.

3 Add the lemon juice and pepper to taste. Blend for a few more seconds.

4 Check for seasoning. According to taste you might like to add more salt or lemon juice. Now is the time to add other flavourings and herbs, too. If the mayonnaise is too thick, add a little boiling water and blend for 2-3 seconds longer.

NOTE This is very simply made basic mayonnaise which can be varied according to personal taste. Try altering the proportions of the oils, or try vegetable oil with a little nut oil. For a less rich sauce mix part mayonnaise with part plain low-fat yogurt.